olas Royle is Professor of English at the University
ssex. His books include the academic bestseller *An
ction to Literature, Criticism and Theory (with
w Bennett), *Telepathy and Literature, The Uncanny,*
ering: A Theory of Literature. He is also the author
ovel, *Quilt*. He is an editor of the *Oxford Literary*

HOW TO READ

SHAKESPEARE

NICHOLAS ROYLE

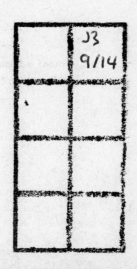

J3
9/14

GRANTA

Granta Publications, 12 Addison Avenue, London W11 4QR

First published in Great Britain by Granta Books 2005
This edition with preface published by Granta Books 2014

A CIP catalogue record for this book
is available from the British Library.

1 3 5 7 9 10 8 6 4 2

ISBN 978 1 78378 029 7
eISBN 978 1 84708 101 0

Typeset by M Rules

Printed and bound by CPI Group (UK) Ltd, Croydon, CR0 4YY

CONTENTS

How am I to read *How to Read*?

This series is based on a very simple, but novel idea. Most beginners' guides to great thinkers and writers offer either potted biographies or condensed summaries of their major works, or perhaps even both. *How to Read*, by contrast, brings the reader face to face with the writing itself in the company of an expert guide. Its starting point is that in order to get close to what a writer is all about, you have to get close to the words they actually use and be shown how to read those words.

Every book in the series is in a way a masterclass in reading. Each author has selected ten or so short extracts from a writer's work and looks at them in detail as a way of revealing their central ideas and thereby opening doors onto a whole world of thought. Sometimes these extracts are arranged chronologically to give a sense of a thinker's development over time, sometimes not. The books are not merely compilations of a thinker's most famous passages, their 'greatest hits', but rather they offer a series of clues or keys that will enable readers to go on and make discoveries of their own. In addition to the texts and readings, each book provides a short biographical chronology and suggestions for further reading and so on. The books in the *How to Read* series don't claim to tell you all you need to know about Freud, Nietzsche and Darwin, or indeed Shakespeare and the

Marquis de Sade, but they do offer the best starting point for further exploration.

Unlike the available second-hand versions of the minds that have shaped our intellectual, cultural, religious, political and scientific landscape, *How to Read* offers a refreshing set of first-hand encounters with those minds. Our hope is that these books will, by turns, instruct, intrigue, embolden, encourage and delight.

Simon Critchley
New School for Social Research, New York

For J.J.
rem acu tetigisti

PREFACE

Creative Reading

This book can hardly hope to live up to its title. There are so many ways to read Shakespeare. In the following pages, however, I try to put the *experience of reading* centre-stage, to suggest how bountiful Shakespeare's writing is in terms of its openness to different readings, and how rewarding it can be to slow down and reflect on some of the astonishing detail of his work. Our understanding of ourselves and other people, language, everyday life, politics, culture, philosophy, non-human animals, religion, love and sex, time and history – to pick out just a few examples – is immeasurably deepened and enriched by reading Shakespeare.

At a time when the study of English in schools and universities seems to be increasingly concerned with the role and importance of creative writing (everyone is a poet at heart, everyone has a novel in her, and so on), my inclination would be to advocate the value of creative reading. Creative reading is not about making things up, reading a line or passage of a text just as it suits us. It has to do with reading closely, paying attention to different possibilities of meaning. No writer in English has as much to tell us about creative reading as Shakespeare. To read his poetry and plays with care, patience and curiosity is a source of intense pleasure. At the same time creative reading entails a sense of the inventive and surprising: 'creative' relates to what is imaginative and original, to an

apprehension of what has never occurred before. There is
something of the atmosphere of *The Tempest*, the 'sea-change'
of which Ariel sings, a metamorphosis of reading or listening
into something 'rich and strange' (1.2.404–5). At such
moments the ghostly substance and beauty of words can
emerge like a new island out of mist. It is as if the reader were
suddenly, mysteriously, encountering the English language for
the first time. *How to Read Shakespeare* attempts to evoke and
explore a few instances of such encounters.

The word 'creative' does not appear in Shakespeare's work.
He could, however, plausibly have used it: according to the
Oxford English Dictionary, 'creative' as an adjective ('Having
the quality of creating, able to create; of or relating to creation;
originative') dates back to 1513. He uses cognate words – such
as *create, created, creating, creation* and *creature* – on plenty of
occasions. Another book would be required to track the force
and effects of Shakespeare's singular deployments of such
words. I would like to comment briefly on just one instance.
Sonnet 81 concludes:

Your monument shall be my gentle verse,   [9]
Which eyes not yet created shall o'er-read,
And tongues to be your being shall rehearse,
When all the breathers of this world are dead;   [12]
  You still shall live (such virtue hath my pen)
  Where breath most breathes, ev'n in the mouths of men.

As elsewhere in the Sonnets (first published in 1609),
Shakespeare's language is dizzying – at once extraordinarily
dense and succinct, playful and grave. We need an annotated
edition of these poems (such as Stephen Booth's) to get a good
grasp of what is going on. The closing six lines (or sestet) of

Sonnet 81 are, on a certain level, breathtakingly arrogant. The friend to whom these lines are addressed may or may not have really existed as a historical individual, but in any case, by a finely fitting irony, the person is not named. The friend is to be remembered, however, thanks to the poet's 'gentle verse'. The 'monument' here is not so much a stone tablet – as the poem's earlier references to 'a common grave' (l.7) and being 'entombèd' (l.8) might indicate – but rather the writing itself. As long as people read this poem, the friend will have 'immortal life' (l.5). Such is the power or 'virtue' of the poet's 'pen'.

What dizzies, above all perhaps, is the sense of an eerie futurity in the moment. Shakespeare invents a marvellous word here, 'breathers' (we are all breathing, creatures that breathe), at the same stroke as evoking the end of the world – when every one of us is dead, 'When all the breathers of this world are dead'. The poem imagines a future time when the speaker and his friend are dead, and indeed everyone now alive is dead, and at the same time invites us to read with 'eyes not yet created' (l.10). This final phrase conjures a bizarre image of reading the future or future readings. It is, in a sense, the ghostly opposite of those human skulls at the bottom of the sea in the marvellous lines about Clarence's dream in *Richard III*, featuring 'holes / Where eyes did once inhabit' (1.4.29–30). Implying Godlike power (only God can create eyes, we may suppose), this image of what is 'not yet created' may helpfully suggest that reading Shakespeare has to do not only with our understanding of the present and the past, but also with kinds of creation still to come. As Theseus, in *A Midsummer Night's Dream*, observes of the imaginative power of poetry: it 'bodies forth / The forms of things unknown' (5.1.14–15).

Nicholas Royle, April 2014

ACKNOWLEDGEMENTS

I have greatly enjoyed talking about various aspects of this book with colleagues at the University of Sussex. In particular I would like to thank Peter Boxall, Brian Cummings, Paul Davies, Mat Dimmock, Andrew Hadfield, Margaret Healy, Alan Sinfield, Céline Surprenant and Keston Sutherland. I am very grateful also to Bella Shand and George Miller at Granta for their careful reading of the original typescript and for their many valuable comments and suggestions.

A NOTE ON TEXTS USED

I have found it helpful to refer to a number of editions of the main plays I discuss in this book. In the following list, the first edition of a given play is the text on which I have principally drawn for quotations and act, scene and line numberings: the New Cambridge *The Merchant of Venice*, ed. M. M. Mahood (updated edn., 2003), the Oxford World's Classics *The Merchant of Venice*, ed. Jay L. Halio (1994), and the Arden *Merchant of Venice*, 2nd series, ed. John Russell Brown (1955); the New Cambridge *Julius Caesar*, ed. Marvin Spevack (1988) (including quotations from North's translation of Plutarch's *Lives of the Noble Grecians and Romans*), the Oxford World's Classics *Julius Caesar*, ed. Arthur Humphreys (1994), the Arden *Julius Caesar*, 2nd series, ed. T. S. Dorsch (1955), and the Arden *Julius Caesar*, 3rd series, ed. David Daniell (1998); the Oxford World's Classics *As You Like It*, ed. Alan Brissenden (1993), the New Cambridge *As You Like It*, ed. Michael Hattaway (2000), and the Arden *As You Like It*, 2nd series, ed. Agnes Latham (1975); the Oxford World's Classics *Hamlet*, ed. G. R. Hibbard (1994), the New Cambridge *Hamlet: Prince of Denmark*, ed. Philip Edwards (updated edn., 2003), and the Arden *Hamlet*, 2nd series, ed. Harold Jenkins (1982); the Arden *Othello*, 3rd series, ed. E. A. J. Honigmann (1999), the New Cambridge *Othello*, ed. Norman Sanders (updated edn. 2003), the Arden *Othello*, 2nd series, ed. M. R.

Ridley (1958), and the Longman New Swan *Othello*, ed.
Gāmini Salgādo (1976); the New Cambridge *Macbeth*, ed.
A. R. Braunmuller (1997), the Arden *Macbeth*, 2nd series, ed.
Kenneth Muir (1951), the Oxford World's Classics *Macbeth*,
ed. Nicholas Brooke (1994), and the Norton Critical Edition
of *Macbeth*, ed. Robert S. Miola (2004); the New Cambridge
Antony and Cleopatra, ed. David Bevington (1990), the Oxford
World's Classics *Anthony and Cleopatra*, ed. Michael Neill
(1994) (including extracts from North's *Plutarch*, from which
I quote), the Arden *Antony and Cleopatra*, 2nd series, ed.
M. R. Ridley (1954) (which includes extensive extracts from
North's *Plutarch* in the original spelling and with original
marginal notes), and the Arden *Antony and Cleopatra*, 3rd
series, ed. John Wilders (1995).

Citations from all other Shakespeare works are based on
The Norton Shakespeare, ed. Stephen Greenblatt, Walter
Cohen, Jean E. Howard and Katharine Eisaman Maus (1997).
For all of the plays discussed here I have found it extremely
helpful to look at the 1623 Folio version (facsimile edition
prepared by Helge Kökeritz, Yale University Press, 1954). I
have also greatly valued being able to explore the 1600
Quarto text of *The Merchant of Venice*, the 1603 and 1604
Quartos of *Hamlet* and the 1622 Quarto of *Othello* (all freely
available, either direct from the British Library website,
www.bl.uk/treasures/shakespeare/homepage.html, or by Googling
'shakespeare in quarto').

INTRODUCTION

POLONIUS   What do you read, my lord?

HAMLET   Words, words, words.

POLONIUS   What is the matter, my lord?

HAMLET   Between who?

POLONIUS   I mean the matter you read, my lord.

                                  (*Hamlet*, 2.2.191–5)

Hamlet, the stage direction tells us, is '*reading on a book*' (2.2.167). They are just words, he suggests, all of them the same, they go on and on and on. The bumbling old Polonius politely asks what the words are about, 'What is the matter, my lord?', but Hamlet apparently misunderstands him. He interprets the word 'matter' in the sense of 'issue' or 'something of concern'. '[Matter] between who?' Hamlet asks. Or in other words: I'm sorry, I was so immersed in my reading, despite the fact that reading is impossible in my current state of deep grief and melancholy, it's all just words, words, words. I didn't realize there was a problem (since my uncle murdered my father, married my mother – it's called incest – and took over from my father as King and pretty much no one seems to think anything of it, why should there be anything the matter, for example between me and the King, or me and all the rest of you? Honestly, I really hadn't noticed there was anything wrong). No, I don't mean that, says Polonius,

'I mean the matter you read.' If we have been reading or watching the play from the start, we know that Hamlet has earlier claimed that he is going to put on 'an antic disposition' (1.5.179), in other words to act in clownish or apparently mad fashion. How 'antic' is he being? How should we read his words? Is Hamlet being funny or deadly serious, calculating or distracted, mocking or indifferent? How might a particular director or actor choose to play him here?

There is something laughable and even crazy about the phrase 'how to read Shakespeare'. William Shakespeare (1564–1616) is probably the most complex, inspiring, challenging and elusive poet and dramatist who ever lived. He wrote many poems, including *Venus and Adonis*, *The Rape of Lucrece*, and 154 sonnets; and many plays (at least 38, a small number of them substantially collaborative), including idiosyncratic kinds of comedy, history, tragedy and romance. In their preface 'To the great Variety of Readers', at the beginning of the first collected edition of *Mr. William Shakespeares Comedies, Histories, & Tragedies* (the book that came to be known as the First Folio or 1623 Folio), his friends and fellow actors John Heminge and Henry Condell offer some simple advice: 'Reade him, therefore; and againe, and againe.' People have been doing this, or trying to do this, ever since. In the space of a short book there is no possibility of even pretending to touch upon the astonishing range or variety of his writings. In the chapters that follow, I aim to look in detail at just seven plays or, more narrowly, at seven shortish passages from seven plays or, in most microscopic fashion of all, at seven words that happen to occur in these seven plays: witsnapper, phantasma, love-shaked, mutes, seel, safe, nod.

I hope that there is, however, a certain method in my madness. (I'm quoting Polonius again, his muttered aside after speaking with Hamlet, 'Though this be madness, yet there is method in't': 2.2.204–5.) I endeavour to move across a number of Shakespeare's plays in what is generally reckoned to be chronological order: *The Merchant of Venice, Julius Caesar, As You Like It, Hamlet, Othello, Macbeth* and *Antony and Cleopatra*. This selection is certainly not intended to be representative of the range of Shakespeare's works; I offer no detailed readings of any of the sonnets or other poems, no histories, no romances. My interest is in deliberately *not* conveying an impression of 'coverage' and, with luck, in provoking readers to go off and explore some of the many texts that do not figure in the discussion. (I confess that the seven plays I have selected here are works I especially love; but I could with great pleasure have selected others.) The seven words I have singled out for close reading are likewise not uniquely special words that sum up Shakespeare's work. I happened upon them, in some respects, by chance; I could very easily have chosen seven others. Yet a detailed attention to such words will, I hope, testify to the incisiveness of Thomas De Quincey's remark, made in 1823, regarding the experience of reading Shakespeare: 'The further we press in our discoveries, the more we shall see proofs of design and self-supporting arrangement where the careless eye had seen nothing but accident.'[1]

My principal aim in this book is to register and explore the *strangeness* of Shakespeare's writing (as we will see, 'strange' is itself a crucial word in his work) – its capacity to surprise and alter our sense of the world. I attempt to track this strangeness as it manifests itself in wordplay, hallucination and fantasy, racial and sexual difference, storytelling, silence and death, the madness and triumph of love, the mind of the psychopathic killer, the magical or telepathic, and the elusive power of ghosts. While I have deliberately avoided miring the discussion in technical details concerning the nature of poetic metre, the iambic pentameter and so on, I read Shakespeare's plays as the work of a poet. My overriding fascination is with the poetic as well as dramatic texture of a given passage, line or turn of words. One of my primary concerns is with trying to elucidate what is going on in a particular word, phrase and passage of Shakespeare, while also trying to acknowledge that paraphrase is itself a kind of madness. As soon as you start trying to *describe in other words* how, for example, 'matter' matters in the exchange between Hamlet and Polonius, you do a kind of violence to the text, no matter how much you may want not to. At the same time, if we cannot rely on the guidance of commentary and paraphrase to get a sense of what is going on when we are faced with the often perplexing or uncertain nature of Shakespeare's words, syntax, idioms and so on, we are lost. He was writing hundreds of years ago and the English language itself has changed in innumerable ways since then, so we all need help. Yet to read Shakespeare it is necessary to be as attentive as possible to what is, or is not, on the page in front of us. In this way it is still possible, I think, to have the feeling of coming to inhabit a line, phrase or word as if absolutely fresh, or even for the first time, after four hundred years or more.

In recent decades the world of Shakespeare studies has given great emphasis to the importance of performance, and the increasing dominance of newer visual media, from TV and film to video, DVD and the Internet, has had an obvious role in this. *How to Read Shakespeare* proceeds in a somewhat different and perhaps unfashionable spirit, focusing above all on the *literary* dimensions of his work. We don't watch a Shakespeare play simply because it is gory and full of murders (though it often is), or because it's about famous people like kings and queens (though it often is), or because it's got lots of love and romance (though it often has). The enduring power of Shakespeare has to do, above all, with the astonishing nature of his language. To appreciate this it is necessary, I believe, to look as carefully as possible at what he actually wrote. This can entail further challenges, as there are many differences or uncertainties over what the text says or should say. I will try, at moments, to explore some of these more scholarly disputes. All of this is not to propose a merely 'linguistic' or 'textual' reading of Shakespeare. His language always calls to be read in terms of something happening – movement, gesture, making, doing. As I hope to make clear, one of the most immediate and profound things about Shakespeare's work is the sense of his love of language – a sense of playing with words and of the amazing, terrifying things that they can do. Words in Shakespeare seem to take on an autonomous life or machine-like power. They are like little search engines, meddling imps, strange creatures with wills of their own.

1

WITSNAPPER

The Merchant of Venice

The Merchant of Venice was probably written around 1596–7 and first published in 1600 as *The Comical History of the Merchant of Venice, or Otherwise Called the Jew of Venice*. This longer version of the title signals a tension between comedy and anti-Semitism that has characterized readings of the play from the start. Shylock is the best-known and most intimately portrayed Jewish character in Shakespeare. A moneylender, he is at the heart of *The Merchant of Venice*, in at least two senses of 'the heart'. This 'Jew of Venice' lends three thousand ducats to the 'Merchant of Venice', a Christian called Antonio, on condition that, if within three months the bond cannot be kept, Shylock is entitled to a pound of Antonio's flesh, to be cut off from his breast, '[n]earest his heart' (4.1.228, 250).

The Merchant of Venice is a shocking play. Shakespeare repeatedly stresses the extent to which Shylock, and other Jews, were subject to abuse, both verbal and physical. The figure of the Jew is identified with that of the dog or 'cur'. This is especially derogatory because dogs were traditionally

regarded, among Jews themselves, as unclean. We learn early
on that Antonio has spat on Shylock and kicked him around
like a stray dog. As Shylock tells him: 'You call me misbeliever,
cut-throat dog, / . . . / You that did void your rheum upon
my beard, / And foot me as you spurn a stranger cur / Over
your threshold' (1.3.103–11). Antonio is pleased to accept
these accusations: 'I am as like to call thee so again, / To spit
on thee again, to spurn thee too' (1.3.122–3). Shylock's word
'stranger' functions in an adjectival fashion, evoking a strange
or stray dog one might kick away from one's door. It resonates
at the same time with other instances of the 'strange' or
'stranger' in Shakespeare's play. *The Merchant of Venice* is about
Christians hating Jews and Jews hating Christians, but it is also
about ethnic, racial and cultural intolerance in more general
ways. It is about the figure of the stranger and the question of
what is 'strange'.

The Merchant of Venice is a strange play, a kind of Janus-
headed work. It opens with Antonio declaring to two fellow
gentlemen of Venice, Salarino and Solanio, that he is sad but
that he does not know why. 'Now by two-headed Janus /
Nature hath framed strange fellows in her time' (1.1.50–1),
says Solanio, in an attempt to evoke, and laugh about, precisely this funny mixture of comedy and tragedy. Besides
Shylock, the other principal character is Portia, a beautiful
young heiress who, in order to obey the peculiar demands of
her father's will, must test prospective suitors by having them
choose from one of three caskets: gold, silver or lead. It is
more the stuff of romance and fairytales, strikingly distinct
from the scenes of Venetian moneylending, commerce and
law (Jew vs. Christian). And yet these different aspects of the
play are at the same time oddly mixed. Among Portia's
numerous suitors is a friend of Antonio's called Bassanio.

Interwoven with the scheme of Shylock's moneylending, then, is the friendship between Antonio and Bassanio. Bassanio is in love with Portia and would like to be among her suitors but lacks 'the means / To hold a rival place with one of them' (1.1.172–3). Antonio borrows from Shylock to provide Bassanio with sufficient funds to woo Portia. Besides Bassanio, all the other suitors are described as 'strangers' (1.2.101–2). Portia's prejudice against a dark-skinned suitor, the Prince of Morocco, is made evident when, even before setting eyes on him, she associates him with having 'the complexion of a devil' (1.2.107) – in the Elizabethan period devils were often conceived as dark-skinned. When the Prince of Morocco does appear, and chooses the wrong casket (gold), she declares as he exits: 'A gentle riddance! . . . / Let all of his complexion choose me so' (2.7.78–9). The Jew, then, is not the only figure of the 'alien' in the play. (The word 'alien' is used at one point, specifically with reference to those who are foreign residents in Venice: see 4.1.349.) At issue are more general questions about what is human and inhuman, natural and strange, and about the very strangeness of language itself.

To recount the plot of a Shakespeare comedy is never simple, but it is also crucial if we are to have a clear sense of the context in which to begin reading a specific excerpt. In Shakespearean comedy the reader or spectator is switched from one kind of scene, one set of characters to another, in an exuberant, relentless, even hectic fashion. Critics talk about a Shakespeare play having a 'sub-plot' and this mode of classification and subordination has traditionally been perceived as helpful in describing how a given play works. The idea of sub-plot is, however, perhaps more strange than natural. The term 'sub-plot' does not appear anywhere in Shakespeare's own writings: it is a sort of critical supplement or afterthought. *The*

Merchant of Venice has a so-called sub-plot involving Shylock's daughter, Jessica, his servant Lancelot the Clown, and a companion of Bassanio's called Lorenzo. But here, as in other Shakespeare plays, what is below or 'sub' the plot is curiously entwined and insidious, as much above or alongside as below the 'main plot'. Lancelot leaves Shylock in order to become Bassanio's man; Jessica, professing herself 'ashamed to be my father's child' (2.3.16), elopes with Lorenzo. Shylock's isolation is thus virtually complete. Lancelot becomes what the stage directions poignantly call 'his man that was' (2.5.0, s.d.), while Jessica summarily tells Shylock: 'I have a father, you a daughter, lost' (2.5.55). Lorenzo and Jessica travel to Belmont and are left in charge of Portia's household while Portia and her waiting-gentlewoman, Nerissa, disguise themselves as men and go to Venice. Portia impersonates a young doctor from Rome called Balthazar, Nerissa his clerk. Portia is able to exploit the fact that she is related to a 'learned doctor' called Bellario, whom the Duke of Venice has requested to advise on the case of Shylock, Antonio and the pound of flesh. Portia's arrival at the courtroom (as Balthazar) is preceded by that of 'his' clerk Nerissa, bearing a letter from Bellario explaining he is sick and recommending the young man Balthazar to stand 'in [his] stead' (4.1.158).

An apparently 'minor' scene in a Shakespeare play can be just as rich and strange, just as illuminating of 'how to read Shakespeare', as a supposedly major scene. Indeed, looking in detail at a 'minor scene' can perhaps more readily lead to a surprising and different appreciation of the play as a whole. With this strategy in mind, I would like to turn to a passage from Act 3 scene 5. At the end of Act 3 scene 4, Portia and Nerissa have left Belmont for Venice, some twenty miles away. Act 3 scene 5 takes place at Belmont in their absence, effectively occupying the time of their journey to Venice. The scene opens with Lancelot the Clown and Jessica: he contends that she is 'damned' because her father is a Jew; she responds that she will be saved by her husband, since he has made her a Christian. Lancelot then jokes about the idea that there are already enough Christians in the world and her husband's having made her a Christian will make bacon impossibly expensive: 'This making of Christians will raise the price of hogs; if we grow all to be pork eaters, we shall not shortly have a rasher on the coals for money' (3.5.17–20). At this point Lorenzo enters.

Enter LORENZO

JESSICA   I'll tell my husband, Lancelot, what you say: here he comes.

LORENZO   I shall grow jealous of you shortly, Lancelot, if you thus get my wife into corners.

JESSICA   Nay, you need not fear us, Lorenzo: Lancelot and I are out. He tells me flatly there's no mercy for me in heaven, because I am a Jew's daughter; and he says you are no good member of the commonwealth, for in converting Jews to Christians you raise the price of pork.

LORENZO   I shall answer that better to the commonwealth than you can the getting up of the Negro's belly: the Moor is with child by you, Lancelot.

LANCELOT   It is much that the Moor should be more than reason; but if she be less than an honest woman, she is indeed more than I took her for.

LORENZO   How every fool can play upon the word! I think the best grace of wit will shortly turn into silence, and discourse grow commendable in none only but parrots. Go in, sirrah, bid them prepare for dinner.

LANCELOT　　That is done, sir; they have all stomachs.

LORENZO　　Goodly Lord, what a witsnapper are you! Then bid them prepare dinner.

LANCELOT　　That is done too, sir; only 'cover' is the word.

LORENZO　　Will you cover then, sir?

LANCELOT　　Not so, sir, neither; I know my duty.

LORENZO　　Yet more quarrelling with occasion! Wilt thou show the whole wealth of thy wit in an instant? I pray thee understand a plain man in his plain meaning: go to thy fellows, bid them cover the table, serve in the meat, and we will come in to dinner.

LANCELOT　　For the table, sir, it shall be served in; for the meat, sir, it shall be covered; for your coming in to dinner, sir, why, let it be as humours and conceits shall govern.　　*Exit*

LORENZO　　O dear discretion, how his words are suited!
　　　　　　　The fool hath planted in his memory
　　　　　　　An army of good words; and I do know
　　　　　　　A many fools that stand in better place,
　　　　　　　Garnished like him, that for a tricksy word
　　　　　　　Defy the matter.

　　　　　　　　　　　　　　　　　　　(3.5.21–58)

The first part of this extract is in the prose form often used by Shakespeare for servants or other so-called 'lowlife' characters. It is only when Lancelot the Clown exits, and Lorenzo and Jessica are alone together, that the text returns to blank verse (at 'O dear discretion . . .'). It is in many ways a peripheral, unremarkable-looking passage, and yet it raises questions that are crucial to a reading of the play as a whole. It prompts us to think about sexuality, the bawdy and the erotic, Jew and Christian, race, class and servitude, economy, wealth and consumption. Above all the passage suggests how 'play[ing] upon the word' is bound up with the way the world works. It invites us to reflect on the question and significance of word-play, of what critics (more or less *all* Shakespeare critics) refer to as puns or quibbles.

How to read Shakespeare is a question of how to think about wordplay. What are the limits of wordplay? Is 'plain meaning' absolutely separable from 'play[ing] upon the word'? Later in the chapter I will consider these issues specifically in terms of the word 'witsnapper', in Lorenzo's phrase 'what a witsnapper are you!' We need to pause first of all, however, on the words 'pun' and 'quibble'. These apparently innocent-looking terms crop up constantly when critics talk about wordplay in Shakespeare. Yet 'pun' and 'quibble' are not Shakespearean words. The only instance of the word 'pun' in Shakespeare is in the sense of the verb 'to pound': 'He would pun thee into shivers with his fist, as a sailor breaks a biscuit' (*Troilus and Cressida*, 2.1.37–8). Likewise, the word 'quibble' appears nowhere in Shakespeare. (According to the *OED*, the first recorded use of 'quibble' is in 1611, and 'pun' in 1662.) I am interested in the question of how to read Shakespeare in new and other ways, without falling back on these traditional but anachronistic critical terms. These terms ('pun' and 'quibble') tend to carry with them a kind of artifi-cial and trivializing effect that is in fact often quite foreign to what is going on in a given passage of Shakespeare. They con-note a certain frivolity, a momentary bubble of fun, something contained and under control, a kind of calculated but ulti-mately pointless exhibition of linguistic playfulness. Moreover they imply that there is a controlling intention – that a partic-ular character is intentionally playing on the meaning of a word. To talk about a character's punning or quibbling is also a way of conveniently forgetting the fact that the character is, in turn, fundamentally Shakespeare's verbal creation: wordplay precedes character. As we will see later in this book, elsewhere in Shakespeare's plays we can find notions of 'double sense' and 'equivocation' (neither of these terms, it may be noted, having the same kind of connotations of frivolity); but strictly and literally speaking, *there are no puns or quibbles in Shakespeare.* The still widespread currency of the 'pun' and 'quibble' in Shakespeare studies perhaps tells us more about his critics than about his own writings.

Critical talk of the 'pun' or 'quibble' stretches back a long way. The most celebrated forefather in this tradition is Dr Johnson who, in his *Preface to Shakespeare* (1765), noted with a mixture of disapproval and pity: 'A quibble is to Shakespeare what luminous vapours are to the traveller; he follows it at all adventures; it is sure to lead him out of his way and sure to engulf him in the mire. It has some malignant power over his mind, and its fascinations are irresistible . . . A quibble, poor and barren as it is, gave him such delight that he was content to purchase it by the sacrifice of reason, propriety, and truth. A quibble was to him the fatal Cleopatra for which he lost the world and was content to lose it.'[2] Johnson would have liked Shakespeare to stop, but he does not stop. And in a sense, in the context of the anachronistic 'pun' or 'quibble', he does not begin. Samuel Beckett's *Murphy* famously declares: 'In the beginning was the pun.'[3] But Shakespeare, in fact, comes before the pun (no pun intended).

Here comes Lorenzo: 'I shall grow jealous of you shortly, Lancelot, if you thus get my wife into corners.' Even or especially when we are engaging with the work on the page, reading Shakespeare is always a question of imagining the scene, how it looks and how it sounds, the body language of the characters, voice, tone and speed. To read Shakespeare it is necessary to project and disseminate ourselves, to try to conceive and figure things from the position of actor or character, as well as director and playwright. We may here imagine Jessica and Lancelot physically close together, in a corner of the stage well away from where Lorenzo enters and perhaps also from us as spectators. Lorenzo will shortly criticize Lancelot's inclination to 'play upon the word'; but there is already play in his own words. 'Corners' in Shakespeare are elsewhere specifically identified with sexual jealousy. In *The Winter's Tale* Leontes suspects his wife Hermione and Polixenes of playing footsie and more: 'Horsing foot on foot? / Skulking in corners? Wishing clocks more swift, / Hours minutes, noon midnight?' (1.2.290–92). Etymologically suggestive of the horns of cuckoldry, 'corner' comes from the Latin *cornu*, 'horn'. 'Corner' in Shakespeare can also signify the female genitals. This sense is hinted at in the description of 'The old fantastical duke of dark corners' in *Measure for Measure* (4.3.164). The various senses appear together in Othello's exclamation, 'I had rather be a toad / And live upon the vapour of a dungeon / Than keep a corner in the thing I love / For others' uses' (*Othello*, 3.3.274–7). Getting his wife into corners and getting it up: we soon discover Lorenzo has grounds for suspecting Lancelot of putting it about and getting in there.

Jessica seeks to put her husband at ease by telling him that she and Lancelot are 'out', that is to say they have quarrelled – though there is also a perhaps less reassuring play on the word 'out' as 'out in the open'. She recapitulates on the argument they had been having about whether a Jew's daughter can ever be anything other than 'damned' (3.5.12) and about Lorenzo himself as an unworthy member of society ('no good member of the commonwealth') because his conversion of

Jessica will help 'raise the price of pork'. In this jesting two of the most serious aspects of Shakespeare's play are mixed: the question of religious difference and the mercantile focus on everything in terms of a 'price'. Lorenzo now makes a surprising announcement: 'I shall answer that better to the commonwealth than you can the getting up of the Negro's belly: the Moor is with child by you, Lancelot.' 'Moor' in Shakespeare's day was a virtual synonym for 'Negro'. Until now there has been no mention in the play of a black servant and we never hear anything else about her. We may suppose Morocco (the rejected suitor of Act 2 scene 7) earlier made a present of a slave girl to Portia's household. So Lorenzo's words may be read: I think you will find I am better answerable to society, Lancelot, than you are, in the light of the fact that you have made the Negro servant pregnant. 'Getting up' suggests both sexually penetrating and impregnating. It also connects with other images of 'growing' in the passage ('I shall grow jealous', 'discourse [will] grow commendable', as well as the more obviously bawdy 'rais[ing] . . . pork', i.e. getting an erection).

It is as if Lancelot's play on 'Moor', and its homophone 'more', has already begun to grow in the 'much': 'It is much that the Moor should be more than reason; but if she be less than an honest woman, she is indeed more than I took her for.' It is significant ('much'), in other words, that she is bigger than is normal ('reasonable'), but to say she is not chaste or respectable ('honest') is a major understatement. There is something quite disturbing and strange about this fleeting discussion of the pregnant black woman. She is apparently worth no more consideration. Yet the very fleetingness of her (non-) appearance here in some respects makes her the more haunting. In particular we might recall her elliptical presence at a crucial moment in the court scene (Act 4 scene 1). This is when Shylock attempts to defend his entitlement to a pound of Antonio's flesh by comparing it with the apparently unquestioned legitimacy of slavery among the Christian 'commonwealth' of Venice:

> You have among you many a purchased slave,
> Which, like your asses and your dogs and mules,
> You use in abject and in slavish parts
> Because you bought them. Shall I say to you,
> 'Let them be free! Marry them to your heirs! . . .'?

(4.1.90–94)

This 'defence' of slavery corresponds with the extraordinary speech Shylock makes earlier about the nature of the Jew: 'I am a Jew. Hath not a Jew eyes? Hath not a Jew hands, organs, dimensions, senses, affections, passions? Fed with the same food, hurt with the same weapons, subject to the same diseases, healed by the same means, warmed and cooled by the same winter and summer as a Christian is?' (3.1.46–50). In each case Shylock questions how society responds to the figure of the stranger, how it reckons with the other (non-Christian, black or Jew), and suggests an alternative thinking of freedom. Shylock's speech, as if in spite of itself, invites us to conceive of society in ways that would be free of what is 'abject' or 'slavish'.

Lorenzo responds to Lancelot's play on 'more' and 'Moor' with an expression of disapprobation: 'How every fool can play upon the word! I think the best grace of wit will shortly turn into silence, and discourse grow commendable in none only but parrots. Go in, sirrah, bid them prepare for dinner.' Playing on words is something to be expected of a clown or fool; but Lorenzo's apparent exasperation extends beyond this, to a sense of any and every fool. He suggests that silence will become the most gracious form of wit ('wit' here bearing the sense of knowledge or wisdom as well as witticism). There is a flashback to his witty description of himself in the opening scene of the play as a 'wise dumb [man]' (1.1.106). Correspondingly, the image of people's speech ('discourse') becoming foolish to the point of merely parrotic takes us back to the Janus-like creatures, evoked by Solanio in the opening scene, who 'will evermore peep through their eyes, / And laugh like parrots at a bagpiper' (1.1.52–3). These 'strange fellows', as Solanio calls them, have their eyes half-shut because they are laughing all the time and they laugh even at what is melancholy. (There is a moment early on in *1 Henry IV* when Falstaff talks of being 'as melancholy . . . as the drone of a Lincolnshire bagpipe': 1.2.65–7.) A single word in Shakespeare, such as 'strange' or 'parrot' or 'melancholy', opens up into a drama of wits, a drama of reading extending across and beyond the text in which it appears. Playing on words, playing with words, words playing all by themselves: wordplay in Shakespeare entails the wit of seeing how no word is exempt.

Thus the word 'witsnapper' is dropped into the proceedings. Lorenzo attempts to restore or at least recall a sense of 'plain meaning': 'Go in, sirrah,' he tells the Clown, 'bid them prepare for dinner.' But this won't work either, as Lancelot plays on the superfluity or ambiguity of the 'for'. Those who are to eat dinner are already prepared, since they already have 'stomachs' (i.e. appetites). Lorenzo tries again, this time omitting the 'for': 'Goodly Lord, what a witsnapper are you! Then bid them prepare dinner.' Lancelot then takes 'cover'. Having introduced the word himself he now chooses to understand it not in the sense of 'laying the table' but of 'putting his hat on'.

'I know my duty,' he says. He knows he should not 'cover' (put his hat on) in the presence of superiors. At another moment in the play the Prince of Arragon, who chooses the silver casket when wooing Portia, imagines a world in which social ranks and positions of authority are not 'derived corruptly', in which 'honour' is based on 'merit': 'How many then should cover that stand bare!' (2.9.41–3). Again, in the play of a single word another conception of society is tacitly inscribed.

'Witsnapper' is a beautiful, strange word: it exists nowhere else in Shakespeare and indeed, according to the *Oxford English Dictionary*, is not recorded anywhere else in the English language before this point. 'Witsnapper' is, apparently, Shakespeare's invention. Elsewhere in his work the snapping of wit is associated with speed. In *Love's Labour's Lost*, for example, wit is evoked in the figure of a sword striking home: 'A sweet touch, a quick venue of wit! Snip, snap, quick and home!' (5.1.51–2). How quickly can or should we read? Shakespeare encourages and accommodates close reading, reading in slow motion; but that closeness is also a matter of going quickly, moving (in Hamlet's phrase) 'with wings as swift / As meditation or the thoughts of love' (1.5.29–30). In a sense, we can never read Shakespeare quick enough, and never speak or write about him quick enough either. 'Speak, breathe, discuss. Brief, short, quick, snap', as the Host exhorts in *The Merry Wives of Windsor* (4.5.1–2). How quickly or how slowly should we read Shakespeare's 'witsnapper'? This verbal invention might even appear to snap together, clamlike, something resembling the beginning and ending of his name, 'Wi[lliam Shakes]per[e]'. Shakespeare's witcraft snaps, snaps at us, snaps us up, knaps us. To knap is to hit (as in *King Lear*, 2.4.125), but also to munch or eat. (The current English word 'knapsack' carries that sense.) 'Witsnapper' might also be wits-knapper, or wit's knapper. At the start of Act 3, Antonio's friends Salarino and Solanio discuss the latest 'news on the Rialto' (3.1.1.). When the loss of Antonio's first ship is disclosed by a 'gossip' woman whom Salarino calls 'Report', Solanio retorts: 'I would she were as lying a gossip in that as ever knapped ginger' (3.1.5–7). It is perhaps not by chance, in this context, that Lancelot's witsnapping has to do with stomachs and appetites, eating and digesting; or that Act 3 scene 5 ends (as we will discover in a moment) with Jessica and Lorenzo witsnapping on these same topics.

There is, apparently, no end – and, more disturbingly perhaps but just as significantly, no beginning – to witsnapping. 'Wit' may primarily refer to humour here, but it can also mean sense, intelligence, imagination, invention, understanding, not to mention both male and female genitals. The snapping might be figurative or literal, funny or painful. To be a witsnapper is apparently to take everything and anything in the wrong sense or at least in a different sense, in other words to be 'quarrelling with occasion'. 'Wilt thou show the whole wealth of thy wit in an instant?' Lorenzo's question suggests that there is something good about holding wit in, about being sparing or restrained in its deployment. It is a question of economy, once again. Lorenzo seems to be rehearsing the role of Dr Johnson, whose disdain for Shakespeare's witsnapping we noted earlier. 'I pray thee understand a plain man in his plain meaning,' Lorenzo tells Lancelot. But what does this mean? We could suggest that there is no plain meaning in Shakespeare without irony, and where there is irony there is no longer any plain meaning. Ironically, as if by a sort of thought transference or mental contagion of words, Lorenzo is here in fact repeating what Lancelot was saying before

Lorenzo entered: 'I was always plain with you' (3.5.3), he tells Jessica at the start of the scene.

At Lancelot's exit Lorenzo's discourse shifts into verse: 'O dear discretion, how his words are suited!' He ironically apostrophizes discrimination ('discretion') as precious ('dear'), again evoking the mercantile language of wealth. Lancelot's words are said to be 'suited' or adapted to the matter in hand and yet they 'defy the matter', as Lorenzo goes on to make clear. 'Play upon the word' is still going on, even if Lorenzo does not say (or even realize) as much. While the sense of 'adapted' is clearly primary, the word 'suited' can also mean 'dressed', as it does earlier in the play when Portia ridicules the English gentleman who comes to woo her: 'How oddly he is suited!' (1.2.60). In Lorenzo's speech this other sense only becomes evident by a sort of deferred effect, a retroactive reading, as we reach the word 'garnished': 'I do know / A many fools that stand in better place, / Garnished like him, that for a tricksy word / Defy the matter.' 'Garnished' means 'dressed' (in terms of clothes) but also 'furnished' (in terms of language). Shakespeare's language is tricksy – ironic, deceptive, artful, ambiguous, crafty or capricious – even when it may appear 'plain'.

Lorenzo then turns to his wife, addressing her as his 'good sweet' (3.5.59). This 'good' is ironic, picking up on the 'army of good words' he has just attributed to Lancelot's memory, while the 'sweet' intimates edibility. Jessica would like to extol her husband's virtues but Lorenzo doesn't want to hear any more, he just wants to go to dinner. Reworking Lancelot's wordplay, Jessica says: 'Nay, let me praise you while I have a stomach' (3.5.75). Playing on the words 'serve' and 'digest', Lorenzo replies: 'No, pray thee, let it serve for table talk; / Then howsoe'er thou speak'st, 'mong other things / I shall digest it' (3.5.76–8). And Jessica's final retort at the end of the scene, 'Well, I'll set you forth' (3.5.78), plays on the sense both of extolling or greatly praising and of dishing up. The scene thus ends with a hint of cannibalism that whets the appetite and knife, anticipating the gruesome dimensions of the court scene that follows.

A few words to finish off, then, concerning Shylock. He loses his case, of course, but his final fate in the court scene (4.1), whereby he is ordered to convert to Christianity, is deeply humiliating, and his abrupt disappearance makes him the greatest after-presence of the play. If the retribution wreaked upon him seems, at least to a contemporary reader or audience, strangely cruel, excessive and unjust, we are also left with a strong impression of Shylock himself as 'strange', strangely strange. At the beginning of the court scene, 'strange' is the crucial word for the Duke in his preliminary summation of Shylock's case:

Shylock, the world thinks, and I think so too,
That thou but leadest this fashion of thy malice
To the last hour of act, and then 'tis thought
Thou'lt show thy mercy and remorse more strange
Than is thy strange apparent cruelty.

(4.1.17–21)

Here the word 'strange' shifts from one sense ('remarkable') to another ('abnormal', 'unnatural'). 'Strange' is haunted by this strange capacity to become a stranger to itself. Portia, disguised as the young Doctor Balthazar, picks up on the word again when first addressing Shylock: 'Of a strange nature is the suit you follow, / Yet in such rule that the Venetian law / Cannot impugn you as you do proceed' (4.1.173–5). The court scene is in many ways in an entirely different tone and register from the passage in Act 3 scene 5 that we have focused on in this chapter, and yet it too turns on wordplay, on the strangeness of witsnapping. It is the witsnapper Portia who prevents Shylock from slicing up Antonio by noting that the bond says a 'pound of flesh' but says nothing about blood:

Take then thy bond, take thou thy pound of flesh,
But in the cutting it, if thou dost shed
One drop of Christian blood, thy lands and goods
Are by the laws of Venice confiscate
Unto the state of Venice.

(4.1.304–8)

As I noted near the outset, *The Merchant of Venice* is a kind of Janus-headed play. In the court scene, as in Act 3 scene 5, we are left with a sense of the disruptive, non-frivolous or uncertainly funny nature of Shakespeare's language. Wordplay or witsnapping makes up the enduringly *strange* character of his writing.

2

PHANTASMA

Julius Caesar

A single word in Shakespeare can provide the spur for a reading of the entire play in which it appears. With this in mind, I want to suggest that what is perhaps most striking about *Julius Caesar* is its shaking of distinctions between being awake and being asleep, its dramatization of the strangeness of time, its ghostliness, its dreamy, hallucinatory qualities – in a word, its sense of 'phantasma'.

Julius Caesar was very likely written in 1599, though it was first published only in 1623, in the First Folio. The play is organized around the historical event of the assassination of Julius Caesar, in 44 BC. The narrative can provisionally be divided into three parts: the build-up, particularly focusing on those conspiring to do the deed (Brutus, Cassius, Casca, Trebonius and others); the event itself (centring on Caesar's '*Et tu, Brute?*': 3.1.77); and then its after-effects, from the extraordinary, crowd-stirring funeral speech by Mark Antony, 'Friends, Romans, countrymen, lend me your ears!' (3.2.65), to the military victory of Antony, Octavius and Lepidus – the

triumvirate in charge of the Roman Empire following
Caesar's murder — over the chief conspirators, Cassius and
Brutus. Cassius finally orders his servant Pindarus to kill him;
Brutus commits suicide.

The word 'phantasma' appears fairly early on in the 'orchard
scene' (Act 2 scene 1). This is the scene in Brutus's orchard
when the conspirators gather to confirm that they will carry
out the assassination. Just before the entrance of the other
conspirators, there is a brief soliloquy in which Brutus says:

> Since Cassius first did whet me against Caesar
> I have not slept.
> Between the acting of a dreadful thing
> And the first motion, all the interim is
> Like a phantasma or a hideous dream.
>
> (2.1.61–5)

The word 'phantasma' does not occur anywhere else in
Shakespeare's writings. It has been variously defined as 'hallucination', 'wild vision' and 'nightmare'. The time of
Shakespeare's play, I would like to suggest, the time of its
happening and the time of its reading, is the time of a phantasma. As we hear more than once in *Julius Caesar*, 'What is't
o'clock?' (2.2.114, 2.4.23). Is it night or day, today or tomor-
row? Am I awake or asleep? Is this a nightmare or
hallucination? And when will the 'phantasma' have stopped?
It is primarily Brutus who thinks and experiences in terms of
'phantasma' but phantasma effects resonate, seep backwards
and forwards, profoundly affecting the question of how we
read the play as a whole.

The 'orchard scene' opens with Brutus trying to wake up
his young attendant, Lucius, wondering what time it is and

wondering when he will ever sleep soundly again: 'I cannot by the progress of the stars / Give guess how near to day. Lucius, I say! / I would it were my fault to sleep so soundly / When, Lucius, when? Awake, I say!' (2.1.2–5). Apparently posed as a question to someone who is not even awake, perhaps the most haunting word here is 'when?' Brutus's invocation of the 'phantasma' or 'hideous dream' occurs just after he has read a paper that has been surreptitiously left in his closet by Cassius, an apparently anonymous letter in which he reads: 'Brutus, thou sleep'st. Awake, and see thyself!' and 'Brutus, thou sleep'st. Awake!' (2.1.46, 48). In his soliloquy Brutus appears to invert this figure of sleep and wakefulness, saying that he has not slept since Cassius 'first did whet' (sharpen, excite, incite) him against Caesar. Yet the syntax of his remark unsettles things further. 'The interim' is itself figured as a hysteron proteron, the rhetorical term for a situation in which what should come after ('the acting' of the 'dreadful thing') is referred to in the speech first, before 'the first motion', the first thought or inward impulse. The 'interim', the time before the assassination, is thus evoked as a phantasma in which time is in reverse.

On the one hand, this sense of the later coming first and the first coming later is in keeping with the play's stress on portents, prophecy and foretelling, on the future shadowing the present. Most memorably, perhaps, there is the soothsayer who tells Caesar to 'beware the Ides [i.e. the 15th] of March' (1.2.18–23), a man whom he dismisses as, ironically enough, a dreamer: 'He is a dreamer, let us leave him' (1.2.24), Caesar declares. Correspondingly, there are the phantasma-like sightings of 'prodigies' and 'portentous things' (1.3.28–31) accompanying the great storm, the 'strange impatience of the heavens' (1.3.61) the night before the assassination.

On the other hand, the sense of the first coming later entails deferral, delayed action or after-effect. There is deferred effect, deferred meaning. The effect and meaning of the assassination take time to become apparent. They become, indeed, apparitional. Caesar is dead before the play is halfway through; yet he is in some respects more present, more active and imposing in the second half of the play than in the first. Shakespeare's play explores the idea that the dead are not as dead as one might like to suppose, especially if (like Brutus) one is answerable for their death. A person can be at least as powerful dead as when alive, and in *Julius Caesar* the dead person goes on demanding answers.

One of the most persistent and literally provoking words in *Julius Caesar* is, indeed, 'answer' (or cognate forms such as 'answered'). In attempting to answer for himself at Caesar's funeral, Brutus declares: 'If . . . any dear friend of Caesar's . . . demand why Brutus rose against Caesar, this is my answer – not that I loved Caesar less, but that I loved Rome more' (3.2.16–20). By way of answer, in his great 'Friends, Romans, countrymen' speech, Antony picks up on this word 'answer', now grimly turning it to the sense of 'pay the penalty for': 'The noble Brutus / Hath told you Caesar was ambitious; / If it were so, it was a grievous fault, / And grievously hath Caesar answered it' (3.2.69–72). The word is then taken up with further deadly force in the following scene, the so-called Cinna episode, in which a group of plebeians, roused to destructive frenzy by Antony's funeral speech, confront a poet and friend of Caesar who happens to have the same name as one of the conspirators ('Cinna'). In menacing fashion they demand that he tell them what is his name, where is he going, where does he live, and is he a married man or a bachelor, and order him to 'Answer every man directly . . . briefly . . .

wisely . . . and truly' (3.3.9–12). We are invited to share with
the poet the paralysing but deadly challenge of having to
answer such an unmanageably multiplicitous demand. He
says he is a bachelor, going to Caesar's funeral, lives near the
Capitol, name is Cinna, not Cinna the conspirator but Cinna
the poet. The plebeians are evidently going to 'tear him
to pieces' (3.3.26) in any case. No answer, it seems, can
save him.

How is one to answer, respond to, or think about *Julius
Caesar*? The most celebrated question in the play, '*Et tu,
Brute?*', might appear to be a rhetorical question, or in any
case a question that Caesar himself answers: '*Et tu, Brute?* –
Then fall, Caesar' (3.1.77). Yet the rest of the play is concerned with how Brutus answers Caesar's question – with
how he responds, how he is answerable, and how he pays
the penalty. It is a question that continues to haunt: literally,
it leads to the appearance of a ghost. The Ghost of Caesar
appears to Brutus in Act 4 scene 3. This is the most
dramatic and explicit instance of a phantasma in the play. It
is also a scene of reading. Brutus is reading – inevitably
prompting thoughts of the reader reading Brutus reading.
In this passage we as readers encounter the idea that the
very act of reading has a capacity for conjuring ghosts.
What is a ghost? How do we respond to or *read* the Ghost
in *Julius Caesar*?

It is night. Brutus is in his tent, in the camp near Sardis. In
Shakespeare's condensed timescale, the Battle of Philippi is
about to occur: the immediately following scene (Act 5 scene 1)
shifts the action to the plains of Philippi. (In fact, Brutus
was at Sardis early in 42 BC, and the Battle of Philippi did not
take place until the autumn.) Others are requested to sleep;
Brutus, as usual, cannot. He tells two of his men, Varrus and

Claudio: 'Lie down, good sirs, / It may be I shall otherwise bethink me' (4.3.250–51). Evidently still subject to a strange vigilance, as he was at the start of the 'orchard scene', he asks his sleepy boy, Lucius, to bring him his book, then to play him some music and sing:

LUCIUS   I have slept, my lord, already.
BRUTUS   It was well done and thou shalt sleep again,
          I will not hold thee long. If I do live
          I will be good to thee.

Music, and a song

          This is a sleepy tune. O murd'rous slumber,
          Layest thou thy leaden mace upon my boy,
          That plays thee music? Gentle knave, good night,
          I will not do thee so much wrong to wake thee.
          If thou dost nod thou break'st thy instrument.
          I'll take it from thee and, good boy, good night.
          Let me see, let me see, is not the leaf turned down
          Where I left reading? Here it is, I think.

Enter the GHOST OF CAESAR

          How ill this taper burns! Ha, who comes here?
          I think it is the weakness of my eyes
          That shapes this monstrous apparition.
          It comes upon me. Art thou any thing?
          Art thou some god, some angel, or some devil,
          That mak'st my blood cold and my hair to stare?
          Speak to me what thou art.
GHOST   Thy evil spirit, Brutus.

BRUTUS	Why com'st thou?
GHOST	To tell thee thou shalt see me at Philippi.
BRUTUS	Well, then I shall see thee again?
GHOST	Ay, at Philippi.
BRUTUS	Why, I will see thee at Philippi then.

[*Exit Ghost*]

Now I have taken heart thou vanishest.

Ill spirit, I would hold more talk with thee.

Boy, Lucius! Varrus! Claudio! Sirs, awake!

Claudio!

LUCIUS	The strings, my lord, are false.
BRUTUS	He thinks he still is at his instrument.

Lucius, awake!

LUCIUS	My lord?
BRUTUS	Didst thou dream, Lucius, that thou so cried'st out?
LUCIUS	My lord, I do not know that I did cry.
BRUTUS	Yes, that thou didst. Didst thou see anything?
LUCIUS	Nothing, my lord.
BRUTUS	Sleep again, Lucius. Sirrah Claudio!

[*To Varrus*] Fellow, thou, awake!

VARRUS	My lord?
CLAUDIO	My lord?
BRUTUS	Why did you so cry out, sirs, in your sleep?
BOTH	Did we, my lord?
BRUTUS	Ay. Saw you anything?
VARRUS	No, my lord, I saw nothing.
CLAUDIO	Nor I, my lord.

(4.3.263–305)

Here as at many other points in the play, Shakespeare's account closely follows Sir Thomas North's translation (published in 1579) of Plutarch's lives of Julius Caesar and Marcus

Brutus. The question of how to read Shakespeare's *Julius Caesar* is intimately bound up with his own reading; this play offers particularly fascinating opportunities for observing instances of how Shakespeare himself read, of how he picked up the words of others, repeated and altered, mimed and made them his own. Most good modern editions of *Julius Caesar* (the Arden, Oxford and New Cambridge, for example) provide extensive excerpts from North's *Plutarch* to facilitate such straightforward but richly illuminating sleuth work.

In the corresponding passage in North's *Plutarch*, we read that 'Brutus was a careful man and slept very little' and that he would often 'read some book till the third watch of the night'. In North's translation the appearance of the ghost is described as follows:

> One night very late, when all the camp took quiet rest, as he was in his tent with a little light, thinking of weighty matters, he thought he heard one come in to him and, casting his eye towards the door of his tent, that he saw a wonderful strange and monstruous shape of a body coming towards him, and said never a word. So Brutus boldly asked what he was, a god or a man, and what cause brought him thither. The spirit answered him: 'I am thy evil spirit, Brutus; and thou shalt see me by the city of Philippes.' Brutus, being no otherwise afraid, replied again unto it: 'Well, then I shall see thee again.' The spirit presently vanished away; and Brutus called his men unto him, who told him that they heard no noise, nor saw anything at all.

It is clear that Shakespeare is indebted to this account in numerous ways, down to the very word or phrase. North's 'thinking of weighty matters' seems to have given Shakespeare the more concentrated, enigmatic and inwardly directed

'I shall otherwise bethink me' (4.3.251). The 'wonderful strange and monstruous shape of a body' in North is transposed to what 'shapes this monstrous apparition'. In North's *Plutarch*, Brutus asks the spirit 'what he was, a god or a man'; in Shakespeare Brutus asks (in similar though also in more Christian and anachronistic fashion), 'Art thou some god, some angel, or some devil . . .?' The words exchanged between Brutus and the 'evil spirit' are almost identical in both texts ('thy evil spirit, Brutus . . . thou shalt see me [at] Philipp[i]', 'Well, then I shall see thee again'), though it is a fascinating detail that the last of these formulations is presented as a question in Shakespeare ('Well, then I shall see thee again?'). There is, in fact, a peculiar unsettling of question and answer. In North we read that '[t]he spirit answered' and then Brutus 'replied again unto it'. The 'again' here is curious, since there was no first reply as such. Does one question a ghost? Or does a ghost question one?

The spirit's vanishing ('vanished away', 'thou vanishest') is in both texts, and Shakespeare also draws on the detail of Brutus then calling his men and discovering 'that they heard no noise, nor saw anything at all'. But there are remarkable differences between the account in North's *Plutarch* and what we find in Shakespeare. Shakespeare's text produces some far more complex and disturbing effects. In North, '[Brutus] thought he heard one come in to him' and, after the spirit vanishes, his men 'told him that they heard no noise'. Shakespeare does something new and profoundly different with this, first of all introducing a new figure, Lucius, who is not in Plutarch at all. There is '*Music, and a song*'; it is 'a sleepy tune', one that sends the player himself to sleep. Brutus says 'murd'rous' (a word which we might indeed reasonably associate with him) not of himself but of sleep or slumber, as if in a strangely transferred epithet, in a beautiful, querying apostrophe: 'O murd'rous slumber, / Layest thou thy leaden mace upon my boy, / That plays thee music?' Slumber is murderous in that it brings about '[t]he death of each day's life': there is an anticipation here of Shakespeare's account, written probably some seven years later, of 'murder[ing] sleep' in *Macbeth* (2.2.35–41). There is also a reference back to a description in Edmund Spenser's *Faerie Queene*: 'Morpheus had with leaden mace / Arrested all that courtly company' (I.iv.44–5). Brutus queries what is happening, as if in indignation, asking how slumber can be arresting the person who is playing music to him: the allusion is to the sergeant or sheriff's officer who places someone under arrest by placing his lead mace on the offender's shoulder. There is a further confusion and uncertainty here as to who ought to be declared or be declaring themselves a murderer. It would appear as if, paradoxically, it is the arresting officer who is 'murd'rous', not the musician. It is as if, in 'sleepy' language, Brutus is playing out some unconscious query that goes back to his contention in the 'orchard scene', that in killing Caesar he and his fellow conspirators 'shall be called purgers, not murderers' (2.1.180).

Slumber does not answer. Brutus takes the instrument away from the sleeping boy, to prevent him from breaking it, and takes up his book '[w]here [he] left reading'. The 'evil spirit' in North becomes, in Shakespeare, specifically 'the Ghost of Caesar', as the stage direction at 4.3.274 makes clear. What signals or accompanies the arrival of this markedly Shakespearean phantasma is not sound but seeing, and more precisely a tricky seeing, an apparition, poor light, a badly burning taper and perhaps the weakness of the haunted man's eyes: there is a stressing of interiority in Shakespeare quite absent from North. We are consistently made aware of the inner world of Brutus's thought, feeling and perception. This sense of interiority is there already in the apparently casual self-referring 'Let me see, let me see', and in the simple but inward-looking 'I think' ('Here it is, I think', 'I think it is the weakness of my eyes'). In Shakespeare, the ghost 'comes upon' Brutus in a strangeness of sleep-enveloping, ill-lit reading. In North, Brutus 'thought he heard one come in to him'; in Shakespeare we *see* one come in to Brutus. As a result it is in a sense we ourselves (as readers or spectators) who are 'left reading', left thinking on the matter of what kind of apparition this is.

'Art thou some god, some angel, or some devil?' asks Brutus. The word 'angel', not in North, occurs on only one other occasion in Shakespeare's play, when, in deep irony, Antony tells the people that 'Brutus, as you know, was Caesar's angel' (3.2.170). 'Angel' shifts between Antony's usage, where it functions primarily in the sense of 'beloved friend' or 'darling', and Brutus's, with its principal meanings of heavenly spirit, guardian spirit or genius. Between these two instances 'angel' also resonates with its more literal force as 'messenger', the meaning of the ancient Greek *angelos*: Caesar's Ghost is indeed a messenger in this respect, come to tell Brutus 'thou shalt see me at Philippi'. Shakespeare's language is angelic: every word is potentially an 'angel', shuttling between appearances, generating new correspondences, a strange messenger in flight across the play. Brutus never heard Antony describe him as Caesar's angel, and yet now the word comes back, intimating that Brutus is still Caesar's messenger, receiving his messages even in death. 'Angel' is thus itself an angel, in the most literal but dreamlike sense, an angelic word or phantasma, strangely communicating between Antony and Brutus, without either being aware of the fact.

Crucial to an understanding of *Julius Caesar* are the workings of the rhetorical figure called prosopopoeia, in which there is an address to or from someone absent or dead. Prosopopoeia is the epitaphic, the voice from the grave or the addressing of the dead. The epitaph on Shakespeare's own grave at Stratford is a fine example of this rhetorical figure: 'Good friend, for Jesus' sake forbear / To dig the dust enclosèd here. / Blessed be the man that spares these stones, / And cursed be he who moves my bones.' The Ghost's speech is prosopopoeia; and so too are various apostrophes to Caesar made, in particular, by Brutus and Antony, after Caesar's death. Thus, for example, in his funeral speech Antony continues to address Caesar as if he is still listening: 'That I did love thee, Caesar, O, 'tis true' (3.1.194). And Brutus repeatedly addresses the man he killed. Near the end of the play, for instance, he declares: 'O Julius Caesar, thou art mighty yet, / Thy spirit walks abroad and turns our swords / In our own proper entrails' (5.3.94–6). In the deadly flatness of the exchange between Brutus and Caesar's Ghost in Act 4 scene 3, it is as if the former no longer has any words of his own, but can only repeat the words of the dead: 'I shall see thee again? . . . Why, I will see thee at Philippi then.' It is only 'now', around the moment of the Ghost's exit, that Brutus starts to feel bold: 'Now I have taken heart thou vanishest.' Shakespeare has evidently transplanted North's 'boldly' ('So Brutus boldly asked . . .') to this point where it is too late, boldness after the event, out of time. This ironic experience of after-the-event or out-of-time is in keeping, however, with the pervasive logic of prosopopoeia. Caesar, or Caesar's Ghost, continues to be addressed, even when no longer present: 'Ill spirit, I would hold more talk with thee.' He haunts Brutus, effectively dictating his life, up to his final words as he runs on his own sword: 'Caesar, now be still, / I killed not thee with half so good a will' (5.5.50–51).

Following the Ghost's exit, Shakespeare does something else quite remarkable with North's *Plutarch*. The initial appearance of the Ghost in Shakespeare is primarily a question of vision and indeed makes it seem very probably a psychological phantasma or hallucination on Brutus's part ('the weakness of my eyes'), whereas North's version describes the initial appearance of the 'evil spirit' in terms of sound (Brutus 'thought he heard one come in to him'). Sound is picked up later in Shakespeare's version, following the Ghost's exit, as Brutus summons his men from their 'murd'rous slumber'. The sense of an overwhelming dissonance is marked by Lucius's crying out that 'The strings . . . are false' (in other words his instrument is out of tune). Shakespeare exacerbates the confusion between wakefulness and dream, the sense of time itself out of time. For the boy, Lucius, it is precisely as if there has been no interruption of the 'sleepy tune'; as Brutus puts it, 'He thinks he is still at his instrument.'

Shakespeare has saved what is perhaps the most eerie effect till last. The Ghost was perhaps not simply in Brutus's own head, after all: Lucius, Varrus and Claudio all claim to have seen nothing, but if Brutus's account is correct they have all cried out in their sleep. Brutus demands of Varrus and Claudio: 'Why did you cry out, sirs, in your sleep?' They answer only with a further question: 'Did we, my lord?' The strangeness of this moment is intensified by Shakespeare's having two characters ('BOTH') say the same thing at the same time 'Did we, my lord?' The sense of mind–reading and the figure of the double (already at issue in the appearance of Caesar's Ghost or Brutus's 'evil spirit') seems to corroborate an impression that the 'phantasma' of Caesar is experienced, consciously or unconsciously, awake or asleep, by everyone. What is a phantasma, in the theatre or on the page, in any case *in the experience of reading*? Isn't the play, in effect, a kind of vast phantasma?

Alongside the cold, ruthless reality of assassination, political ambition, treachery and suicide, Shakespeare's *Julius Caesar* never lets up on the strange sense that, in the words of Prospero, 'We are such stuff / As dreams are made on' (*The Tempest*, 4.1.156–7). The play generates a peculiar sort of double perspective, the experience of what, in a memorable phrase, Cicero calls 'a strange-disposèd time' (1.3.33). *Julius Caesar* leaves us with an especially strong impression of wakefulness, to the point of insomnia. This sleeplessness is epitomized by Brutus and perhaps inevitably comes to be associated with guilt as much as ruthlessness. At the same time, however, Shakespeare's play seems to envelop a singularly nightmarish world of its own, rendering to itself a hideous dreamtime.

3

LOVE-SHAKED

As You Like It

As You Like It is generally thought to have been written between 1599 and 1600, although it was not published until 1623, in the First Folio, and indeed there is no definite record of performance before 1740. As its title suggests, the play is concerned with desire. It is both simple, light, straightforward, and not. Consider the little word 'as', complex and deceptive from the start. It is not only the first word of the title but the first word of the play as well: 'As I remember,' it begins. We (who may like to think of ourselves as the 'you' referred to in the title) might choose to read the 'as' as a 'because', 'since', 'while' or 'when', but are perhaps more likely to read it as 'in the way that', 'to whatever extent', 'in whatever proportion'. The latter reading still entails uncertainty. Does 'as' involve something complete and whole ('just as', 'in just the way that') or not ('only to the extent or in the proportion that')? There is irreducible ambiguity here, whether we like it or not. Is the 'it' of the title the world or life? Or does 'it' refer to the play itself, or indeed the title? *As You Like It* is very much a play about itself, and about the limits (or not) of the stage. This is the play, after all, in which we find the great speech from the melancholy Jaques (to be variously pronounced 'Jakus', 'Jakwis' or, in Shakespeare's more lavatorial humour, 'Jakes', i.e. 'a privy') that begins: 'All the world's a stage, / And all the men and women merely players' (2.7.139–40). 'Merely' here means 'purely' and is a word I will come back to. *As You Like It* is a masterpiece of lightness that is also a profound meditation on the nature of acting and the stage, playing and dissimulation. It shows how deeply desire and love are caught up in language, and dramatizes the pleasures as well as the anguish and strangeness of being a 'player'.

At the heart of *As You Like It* is the love between Rosalind and Orlando. She is the daughter of Duke Senior, a good man who has been deposed by his younger brother, Frederick. Banished from the court, Duke Senior has gone to 'the forest of Arden, and a many merry men with him; and there they live like the old Robin Hood of England' (1.1.109–11). (The Forest of Arden is supposed to be in France, though it also happens to have been the name of a forest near Shakespeare's hometown of Stratford.) Orlando is the youngest son of Sir Rowland de Boys, now deceased but formerly one of Duke Senior's most loyal supporters. In accordance with contemporary English law, Orlando's eldest brother Oliver inherited all the family wealth on their father's death. Oliver was also charged with looking after young Orlando's education, a duty he has neglected. Rosalind stays at the court principally on account of her close friendship with her cousin, Duke Frederick's daughter Celia. We are told that 'never two ladies loved as they do' (1.1.106–7), but then Rosalind meets Orlando and it is, evidently, mutual love at first sight. Shortly after this the usurping Duke, apparently of the view that his niece's positive standing among 'the people' (1.3.77) is working at the expense of his daughter's, banishes Rosalind along with her father. Celia chooses to go with her beloved cousin and live in the forest. Rosalind dresses as a young man, disguising herself as a shepherd called Ganymede, while Celia becomes a shepherdess, Ganymede's sister Aliena. Likewise Orlando is compelled to flee from the increasingly violent Oliver. As the old family servant Adam tells him: 'this night he means / To burn the lodging where you use to lie, / And you within it' (2.3.23–5). Orlando, then, also takes off for the forest.

The plot of Shakespeare's *As You Like It*, mostly based on Thomas Lodge's popular novel *Rosalynde* (1590), focuses on love and sexual desire, but also turns on the importance of religious or similar conversion. Duke Frederick meets an old religious man on the outskirts of the forest and becomes a 'convertite' (5.4.179), whereupon he hands back his crown and lands to Duke Senior, enabling his banished brother finally to return to the world of the court. Oliver, who gets into a scrape with a snake and a hungry lioness in the forest and is saved by his brother, Orlando, experiences a 'conversion' (4.3.137) to brotherly love and reconciliation. Romantic love seems similarly sudden and dramatic. Oliver also falls in love with Celia (or rather Aliena) at first sight. Looking, it seems, is enough to turn 'like' to 'love': 'Is't possible that on so little acquaintance you should like her? That but seeing, you should love her?', as Orlando puts it (5.2.1–2). And Celia likewise falls in love with Oliver. The play ends with no fewer than four marriages (Rosalind and Orlando, Celia and Oliver, a shepherd called Silvius and shepherdess called Phoebe, and the court jester Touchstone and Audrey, a goatherd). The final scene, then, is of 'rustic revelry' (5.4.172), celebration and song.

If the world of the play is pervasively that of a 'golden world' (1.1.113), a world of romance and fantasy, it is also a stage on which we witness intricate and unsettling explorations of the nature of love, self and language. The key player in these explorations is Rosalind, as we can see from a passage in the middle of the play, shortly after Orlando first re-encounters her, now disguised as the shepherd Ganymede. Orlando has been wandering lovelorn through the woods, carving her name on the barks of trees and leaving love poetry hanging from the branches. One of these poems starts: 'From the east to western Ind / No jewel is like Rosalind' (3.2.84–5). But what is Rosalind 'like', in truth? In the dialogue that follows we encounter a strange cocktail of possible answers, along with some provocative suggestions regarding the nature of love and desire.

ROSALIND There is a man haunts the forest that abuses our young plants with carving 'Rosalind' on their barks; hangs odes upon hawthorns and elegies on brambles; all, forsooth, deifying the name of Rosalind. If I could meet that fancy-monger, I would give him some good counsel, for he seems to have the quotidian of love upon him.

ORLANDO I am he that is so love-shaked. I pray you, tell me your remedy.

ROSALIND There is none of my uncle's marks upon you. He taught me how to know a man in love, in which cage of rushes I am sure you are not prisoner.

ORLANDO What were his marks?

ROSALIND A lean cheek, which you have not; a blue eye and sunken, which you have not; an unquestionable spirit, which you have not; a beard neglected, which you have not – but I pardon you for that, for simply your having in beard is a younger brother's revenue. Then your hose should be ungartered, your bonnet unbanded, your sleeve unbuttoned, your shoe untied, and everything about you demonstrating a careless desolation. But you are no such man. You are rather point-device in your accoutrements, as loving yourself than seeming the lover of any other.

ORLANDO Fair youth, I would I could make thee believe I love.

ROSALIND Me believe it? You may as soon make her that you love believe it, which I warrant she is apter to do than to confess she does. That is one of the points in the which women still give the lie to their consciences. But in good sooth, are you he that hangs the verses on the trees wherein Rosalind is so admired?

ORLANDO I swear to thee, youth, by the white hand of Rosalind, I am that he, that unfortunate he.

ROSALIND But are you so much in love as your rhymes speak?

ORLANDO Neither rhyme nor reason can express how much.

ROSALIND Love is merely a madness, and I tell you, deserves as well a dark house and a whip as madmen do; and the reason why they are not so punished and cured is that the lunacy is so ordinary that the whippers are in love too. Yet I profess curing it by counsel.

ORLANDO Did you ever cure any so?

ROSALIND Yes, one; and in this manner. He was to imagine me his love, his mistress; and I set him every day to woo me. At which time would I, being but a moonish youth, grieve, be effeminate, changeable, longing and liking, proud, fantastical, apish, shallow, inconstant, full of tears, full of smiles; for every passion something, and for no passion truly anything, as boys and women are for the most part cattle of this colour – would now like him, now loathe him; then entertain him, then forswear him; now weep for

him, then spit at him, that I drave my suitor from his mad
humour of love to a living humour of madness, which was
to forswear the full stream of the world and to live in a
nook merely monastic. And thus I cured him, and this
way will I take upon me to wash your liver as clean as a
sound sheep's heart, that there shall not be one spot of
love in't.

ORLANDO   I would not be cured, youth.

ROSALIND   I would cure you if you would but call me Rosalind and
come every day to my cot, and woo me.

ORLANDO   Now by the faith of my love, I will. Tell me where it is.

ROSALIND   Go with me to it, and I'll show it you. And by the way you
shall tell me where in the forest you live. Will you go?

ORLANDO   With all my heart, good youth.

ROSALIND   Nay, you must call me Rosalind. – Come, sister. Will you
go?

Exeunt

(3.2.343–414)

This is, in effect, a seduction scene, a delectable leading
astray. Rosalind, as Ganymede, persuades Orlando to go off
with him and make believe that he, Ganymede, is Rosalind.
Everything in the passage works through the seductiveness of
dissimulation and play. It is about the romantic rapport
between Rosalind and Orlando, and our pleasure in knowing what Orlando apparently does not. We know that
Ganymede is Rosalind, that Rosalind knows that Orlando is
the person who has been carving her name and writing love
poetry ('odes' and poems in elegiac metre or 'elegies'), and
that she knows very well that he is in love with her. The
passage is also intensely homoerotic, however, primarily concerning a relationship between a man, Orlando, and a boy, the

'fair youth' Ganymede, but also between two women. The
dialogue is between Ganymede, or Rosalind, and Orlando,
but as the final words of the scene make clear, Celia, disguised
as Aliena, is also present: 'Come, sister.' (It may be that the
melancholy lord, Jaques, is also present, lingering eaves-
droopishly at the edge of the stage, throughout these final
lines of Act 3 scene 2: he enters with Orlando at line 242
and, in the 1623 Folio text, there is no stage direction for
his exit.)

In the opening scenes of the play, the love between
Rosalind and Celia is described as 'dearer than the natural
bond of sisters' (1.2.261). While they lived in the world of the
court they 'slept together, / Rose at an instant, learned,
played, eat together'. They were, in Celia's words, 'like Juno's
swans . . . coupled and inseparable' (1.3.71–4). The erotic
poignancy of this passage in Act 3 has to do in part with
Celia's silence, Aliena's alienation. She can no longer think, as
she did at court, that 'thou [Rosalind] and I are one' (1.3.96);
Orlando has altered all of that. Despite the fact that these
women are still together, one of them cross-dressing, living as
brother and sister in the forest, this scene marks an important
transition in their relationship. In her remarks to Orlando,
Rosalind is also providing Celia with a sort of lesson in love.
As Rosalind acutely understands, 'The sight of lovers feedeth
those in love' (3.4.52). Love is deeply bound up with a logic
of mimicry and substitution. This passage in Act 3 scene 2 is
preparing Celia (and us) for her falling in love with Oliver
later in the play.

Shakespeare would have written Celia–Aliena's part imagining it to be played by a boy. In many ways the erotic power
of the passage has to do with love between men or boys, or
between a man and boy. Rosalind's chosen name, 'Ganymede',

refers to the beautiful boy carried off by Jupiter and made to
serve as his cupbearer, but it was also a sixteenth-century
synonym for 'catamite', a 'boy kept for homosexual purposes'
as *Chambers* dictionary puts it. Whether or not Orlando sees
through Ganymede's disguise might depend on how a given
director or actor chooses to play it. Is Orlando dissimulating
as well? More obviously we must wonder, is this passage
about the seductive power of a young woman or a young
man? Shakespeare's text is beautifully promiscuous in these
respects. We may here recall Oscar Wilde's insight, from *The
Importance of Being Earnest*, that 'the essence of romance is
uncertainty'. The part of Rosalind, in Shakespeare's time,
was of course played by a boy, no doubt a 'pretty youth' (in
Orlando's phrase: 3.2.321). *As You Like It* concludes with
an epilogue in which Rosalind addresses the audience and
explicitly draws attention to the fact that she is a boy: 'If I
were a woman I would kiss as many of you as had beards
that pleased me, complexions that liked me, and breaths
that I defied not' (Epilogue, 16–19). Shakespeare generates
a giddily, entrancingly uncertain play of substitutions. There
would seem to be something for everyone – depending on
what you fancy. Shakespeare has it more than both ways: love
between women, men and boys, men and women, boys as
women, women as boys, boys playing women playing boys
playing women, and so on, as you like it.

Rosalind as Ganymede plays the part of someone who does
not know Orlando, who finds the poetic attempts at 'deifying
the name of Rosalind' laughable, and who is willing to give
some good advice to the 'fancy-monger', the dealer in love or
purveyor of fantasies who has been 'abus[ing] our young
plants'. She *acts* willing, that is, so long as she can be convinced
she is truly addressing the fancy-monger in question. Rosalind

(and the play) is playing with the simple but perhaps unfathomable question: how can I be sure that you are in love? At the same time, the undersense of the language here is lewdly suggestive. 'Cunt', it may appear, is never far from Shakespeare's lips, especially when words containing 'con' or 'coun' are in play. We are deep in what Hamlet calls 'country matters' (3.2.103). But 'cunt' is also never present: the word could not be used on the public stage. 'If I could meet that fancy-monger, I would give him some good counsel, for he seems to have the quotidian of love upon him.' The man in question is right in front of her: here is the pleasure of playing about with recognition and non-recognition, the reader and speaker (Ganymede–Rosalind) conning more, being better counselled than the listener (Orlando). Orlando is not well; he would benefit from some of this counsel. 'Quotidian', literally 'daily', refers to a fever that recurs every day, an ague or similar attack of continuous shivering: such is the affliction called love.

Picking up on this sense of a fit or fever, Orlando then confesses: 'I am he that is so love-shaked.' This lovely compound occurs nowhere else in Shakespeare. 'Love-shaked' is what is known as a nonce-word, a word that is a one-off, a product of the spur or shake of the moment. It is perhaps not surprising that someone with a name like 'Shakespeare' should have a penchant for 'shake'-words. It may be fitting to recall in this context Robert Greene's famous snide remark about Shakespeare in 1592 as the young poet who is 'in his owne conceit the onely Shake-scene in a countrie' (see *Norton Shakespeare*, p. 3322). With or without a lewd play on 'conceit' (here primarily meaning 'imagination') and 'countrie', Greene appears to be piling up the insults. To shake can also mean to insult or verbally abuse. Thus in the opening scene of *As You Like It*, Orlando tells the servant Adam to withdraw so that he can 'hear how [Oliver] will shake me up' (1.1.25–6). The story of Orlando takes him from a life of shaking up by his wicked brother to being love-shaked by Rosalind. 'Shaked' is not the same as 'shaken'. We can compare the opening words of *1 Henry IV* (1596–7), in which the King begins, 'So shaken as we are, so wan with care . . .' (1.1.1), with the description of the ailing Falstaff in *Henry V* (1598–9) as 'so shaked of a burning quotidian-tertian, that it is most lamentable to behold' (2.1.107–8). Henry IV's self-description indicates stability within the shaking, a sense that the shaking has an end. 'Shaked', by contrast, suggests a shaking that is still going on, an unpredictable, dangerous, continuing disturbance. The feverishness of the 'shaked' in *Henry V* is such that it shakes the distinction between the 'quotidian' (everyday) and the 'tertian' (a fever that recurs every third day). To be 'love-shaked' is quite different from being 'love-shaken'.

With this 'shaked' in mind we might venture a nonce-word of our own. There has been much talk, down the centuries, of Shakespearean language, but it would perhaps be appropriate to think equally of Shakespeared language – of the sudden, often completely new twists and turns given to language in Shakespeare's works. *As You Like It* contains many words that are either defined as nonce-words (like 'love-shaked') or being used in an apparently new, previously unrecorded sense (such as 'elegies' as love poems rather than as lamentations: 3.2.345). To speak of Shakespeared language is to suggest something of this suddenness, a sort of fixed or 'speared' but continuously provoking inventiveness. In the passage in Act 3 scene 2 of *As You Like It*, love is figured as a dangerous illness for which the afflicted

Orlando requests a remedy: 'I am he that is so love-shaked.
I pray you, tell me your remedy.' Ganymede–Rosalind has
earlier claimed to have had an old religious uncle who knew
all about love and whom s/he heard 'read many lectures
against it' (3.2.332–3). ('Lecture' here as 'admonitory speech'
is another case of a word being used in this particular sense
apparently for the first time.) He taught Ganymede–Rosalind
'how to know a man in love'. Orlando is no such man: 'There
is none of my uncle's marks upon you.' Love is wittily con-
strued as something to be seen, having visible 'marks' such
as would be associated with a fever or witchcraft. Country
sweethearts in Shakespeare's time exchanged rings plaited
from rushes. Alluding to love as flimsy and easily broken out
of, Rosalind concludes: 'In which cage of rushes I am sure
you are not prisoner.' Asked what are the marks of a man
in love, she then regales Orlando with a rapid satirical
inventory of a stereotypical Elizabethan melancholy lover:
thin ('a lean cheek'); rings under the eyes ('blue' and 'sunken')
from sleeplessness; taciturn, impatient, not inclined to answer
any questions (having 'an unquestionable spirit'); an un-
kempt beard; and clothes in disarray, suggestive of a general
state of 'careless desolation'. She ends by declaring that
Orlando is indeed so fastidiously precise in his dress (so
'point-device in [his] accoutrements') that he looks more
in love with himself than with anyone else. Rosalind
seems to understand, as well as anyone in Shakespeare, the
disturbing but compelling ways in which love is narcissistic.
Her quip at Orlando calls to mind Nietzsche's celebrated
aphorism: 'In the end one loves one's desire and not what
is desired.'[4]

In Rosalind's speech, what I called a moment ago Shakespeared language is also displayed in the sense of discourse as

discovery, speech as adventure. You can never be sure quite
how a character is going to say something but, more remarkably, you have the feeling the character is equally capable of
being taken by surprise. In this list of 'accoutrements' that
Orlando does not have, Ganymede–Rosalind mentions 'a
beard neglected, which you have not', then pauses, as if everything could or perhaps must give way at this point. Rosalind
need not say anything more about the beard but something
leads her on, beyond what is proper or prudent, into a space
of discourse that is unexpectedly dangerous and exhilarating:
'a beard neglected, which you have not – but I pardon you for
that, for simply your having in beard is a younger brother's
revenue.' But I forgive you for that, she says, the size and
nature of your beard is like a younger brother's income or
inheritance, in other words paltry. The introduction of the
question of the 'younger brother's revenue' strains at the
limits. Rosalind plays dangerously close with losing her
identity as Ganymede, a shepherd who would not be
expected to know or care very much about inheritance law,
and certainly not be aware of the fact that Orlando is just such
a younger brother.

Yet this chancy, seemingly uncontrollable outpouring
transfixes us just as much as it does any character on the
stage. Perhaps the most enchantingly loquacious, seductively
directive character in Shakespeare, Rosalind is unstoppable.
She has indeed more lines than any other female character in
Shakespeare's plays, and already by this point in the passage
it is striking how much more she has to say than does (or
can) the love-shaked Orlando. He need only remark that he
would really like this pretty young man to believe that he is
in love – and Rosalind launches off, dazzling, once more.
'Me believe it? You may as soon make her that you love

believe it, which I warrant she is apter to do than to confess she does. That is one of the points in the which women still give the lie to their consciences.' Rosalind plays again here on our knowing that 'me' and 'she' are one: 'as soon' would be absolutely accurate, a fine example of 'point-device' speech. The 'fair youth' Ganymede then remarks that 'her that you love' (a formulation in which, we may note, a little ground appears to be tacitly conceded to Orlando) is more prone to believe a declaration of love than she would admit to.

Rosalind at once meditates and plays on the performative capacity of language, the power of language not only to describe but to do something through the act of saying. To say 'I warrant', 'I confess' or 'I profess' ('I profess curing it', as Rosalind later says) is a form of pledge or promise, a commitment made through the act of speaking. Likewise 'I love you' is a performative: it is a form of pledge or promise. Love, as *As You Like It* demonstrates, is dizzyingly dependent on the performative effects of language, on what is at once scripted and uncertain. In saying 'I love you' it is always possible that the speaker is lying, or in other words acting. This is one reason why Orlando's beloved might not be willing to 'confess' she believes him. In keeping quiet about their credulity women are always showing the falsity of ('still giv[ing] the lie to') their innermost thoughts and feelings ('consciences'). The young shepherd Ganymede, who would perhaps not be expected to have any great understanding of women, transports us into an extraordinary female interiority, suggesting that the performative power of language ('giv[ing] the lie') lies at the very heart of their thinking. Within their 'consciences', women are still manipulating and being manipulated by this power. To 'give the lie' is a performative: it is to prove wrong or openly accuse of falsehood. But Ganymede–Rosalind's words are also playing or performing in other, more bawdy ways. To 'give the lie' carries a sexual connotation corresponding to the Clown's proposition in *Antony and Cleopatra*: 'A very honest woman, but something given to lie' (5.2.25–6). Shakespeare often plays on this double sense of 'lie', as in Sonnet 138: 'Therefore I lie with her, and she with me, / And in our faults by lies we flattered be.' Finally, the sexual 'give' in Ganymede's words (which might, on stage, be accompanied by some lewd gesture) is further concentrated in the word 'consciences' which, once again, plays on 'cunt'. This, we might venture, is language remarkably far up itself.

'But in good sooth, are you he that hangs the verses on the trees . . .?', Ganymede–Rosalind goes on, as if to mark a return to complete seriousness and truth ('good sooth'). As readers or spectators we are encouraged to believe in the love between Orlando and Rosalind, at the same time as being kept acutely aware of the extent to which everything is theatrical, rhetorical, made up. Orlando's response ('I swear . . . I am that he, that unfortunate he') cannot be unduly hammed up. It is important for the actor (and likewise the reader or spectator) to maintain a balance: to be 'love-shaked' is not simply to be an object of satire or derision. Orlando is, after all, the man who has, in Celia's words, 'tripped up . . . [Rosalind's] heart' (3.2.204–5). At the same time, it is possible, and perhaps even irresistible, to see this scene of the play, and in particular to see Rosalind's intensely seductive wordplay and play-acting, as part of an educative process (helped on by a fictional 'uncle') to bring Orlando to a new and different conception of love, less melancholy, at once more balanced and more playful. As Rosalind elsewhere acknowledges: 'Men have died from time to time, and worms have eaten them, but not for love' (4.1.97–8).

So how do you measure love? 'Neither rhyme nor reason can express how much' Orlando is in love. 'Neither rhyme nor reason' was already proverbial in Shakespeare's time, but here of course it is playfully literal. Orlando's rhymes, his 'odes' and 'elegies', cannot express his love. Neither can a discourse of 'reason'. Love may be declared, sworn or promised in words, and this performative force of language may even engender love, but even so love is beyond all words, beyond all measure. In which case, as Rosalind immediately pursues, it is 'merely a madness'. Love is absolutely mad. This sense of 'merely' recalls Jaques's 'All the world's a stage, / And all the men and women merely players'. Living is nothing but playing, and love nothing but madness. Love, including a love of writing and reading love poetry (not stopping short perhaps at that long and astonishing love poem called *As You Like It*), is merely a madness.

There is a powerful switch here in the tone of the passage, as we are invited into a horrible darkness. Love, the handsome young shepherd tells Orlando, 'deserves as well a dark house and a whip as madmen do'. The allusion here is to the contemporary practice of confining those perceived to be insane in a dark room and whipping them to rid them of the devils by which they were thought to be possessed. Ganymede–Rosalind then picks up Orlando's use of the word 'reason' and makes a lunacy of it: the reason why lovers are not treated in this way, she suggests, is that the whippers are in love as well. The darkness of this image spreads, like the moment with the Cheshire Cat in *Alice in Wonderland*: 'We're all mad here. I'm mad. You're mad.'[5] All apparently except

Rosalind, cross-dressed as a shepherd: 'I profess curing it by counsel.' Asked by Orlando if s/he ever successfully cured anyone, the shepherd says, 'Yes, one.' This one person was cured by having to imagine that Ganymede was really a woman, 'his mistress', and by having to woo her every day. The only way out of madness is to act, play the part of someone else, exchange one madness for another. Thus the woman, Rosalind, who is acting the man, Ganymede, acts a woman – a mimicking of the fickle and uncaring mistress made famous by the love poetry of Petrarch (1304–74) – and drives her 'suitor' out of the state of being madly in love ('the mad humour of love') into the actual state (the 'living humour') of madness. This play-acting 'mistress', no longer 'merely' Rosalind nor Ganymede, is a Shakespeared creation, love-shaked, conjured in words on the spur of the moment. This imaginary mistress is 'a moonish youth', in other words as inconstant and changeable as the moon, indeed literally lunatic: 'moonish' refers back to the word 'lunacy' which derives from the Latin *luna* meaning 'moon'.

Rosalind's speech is hectic and exhausting. The sentence starting 'At which time would I, being but a moonish youth. . .' makes for one of the longest sentences in Shakespeare. Halting with the image of 'a nook merely monastic' (a life of completely religious seclusion) as the only apparent alternative to being madly in love, Rosalind summarizes by saying that she can take Orlando's liver (then thought of as the seat of the passions) and wash every 'spot of love' off it. The image of making his liver 'as clean as a sound sheep's heart' reminds us of Ganymede's occupation as shepherd in the forest. The brevity of Orlando's reply at the end of this long speech from Rosalind is at once funny and moving: 'I would not be cured, youth.' But equally startling is the speed with which she then manages to get Orlando to agree to engage in the play-acting and come to her each day to woo him: 'I would cure you if you would but call me Rosalind and come every day to my cot, and woo me.' It would appear that merely the name 'Rosalind', and the chance to call him by that name, are enough to persuade Orlando, without further ado, to woo 'her'. He promises to go 'With all my heart, good youth' – and Orlando might at this point make some hearty mannish gesture (such as a slap on the back) – giving rise to Ganymede's 'Nay, you must call me Rosalind.'

And so the play goes on, as if supervised or overlooked from within by the extraordinary figure of Rosalind. I borrow 'overlooked' from *The Merchant of Venice* when Portia confesses to her feeling that Bassanio's eyes have 'o'erlooked [her]' (3.2.15), in other words bewitched her. Rosalind is like a figure of the playwright or director within the play. It is she above all who 'can do strange things' (5.2.57), shaping and shaking what is to be made of 'love', both among characters in the play and among ourselves as readers or spectators. In the context of the 'rustic revelry', dancing and harmony of the play's conclusion, it is tempting to see the melancholy Jaques as the only counterforce to the light concerns of the play: 'So to your pleasures,' he avers, 'I am for other than for dancing measures' (5.4.176–7). But the wonderfully airy nature of Shakespeare's comedy is deceptive. Through the ceaselessly inventive and seductive effects of Shakespeared language we are left pondering strange thoughts and feelings. What we might understand by 'love' is indeed, in various ways, shaked in the light of this play. In particular we are given to suppose that it is indissociably bound up with a sense of being programmed. Love appears to be inseparable from a logic of imitation, and at the same time 'merely a madness'. When or where, after all, does the play or playing end? How could we ever be certain that we are not, as Jaques says, 'merely players', shifting through this 'strange, eventful history' (2.7.164) he calls life?

4

MUTES
Hamlet

What happens when you die? And how, if at all, will you be remembered? *Hamlet* (1600–1601) offers perhaps the most concentrated and haunting exploration of such questions anywhere in the history of Western literature or philosophy. Many famous phrases that people know from Shakespeare come from *Hamlet*. These would include 'in my mind's eye' (1.2.185), 'to be, or not to be' (3.1.57), 'shuffle off this mortal coil' (3.1.68), 'hoist with his own petard' (3.4.190) and 'the rest is silence' (5.2.311). It is perhaps not by chance that the first of these is about seeing a dead person or ghost, and the last four specifically about dying. Hamlet, of course, is not real; but in some ways we may feel we know him better than we do most of the real people we meet. It is from his mouth that we receive all five of the phrases just listed. When Hamlet speaks his famous last words, 'the rest is silence', we understand 'rest' primarily as 'remainder' or 'what is left'. Is the rest really silence? Does even a day go by without someone (or indeed perhaps hundreds of people) ventriloquizing him?

Hamlet's last words are far from being the last words on Hamlet. Even the apparently straightforward word 'rest' will not rest. Another sense of 'rest', as 'repose', including the biggest repose of all ('death'), is invoked by Horatio in the lines immediately following: 'Good night, sweet prince, / And flights of angels sing thee to thy rest' (5.2.338–9). Do they? Is Hamlet at rest? Where? When? Shakespeare's play is in a sense all about a man (Hamlet) entreating a ghost (the Ghost of the King, his murdered father) to 'Rest, rest, perturbèd spirit' (1.5.190). Of all Shakespeare's works, Hamlet is perhaps the least restful – the most deeply unsettling, 'out of joint' (1.5.196) and disturbing.

The sense of restlessness and unease might well begin with the question of which version of Hamlet we should be reading (or watching). There are basically three versions of the text, the first published in 1603, known as the 'bad quarto', a comparatively short text (2,200 lines), full of what look like misremembered or otherwise erroneous construals of the text, compared with the version known as the Second Quarto, published the following year in 1604. The Second Quarto is 3,800 lines long and is generally reckoned to have been based on Shakespeare's own handwritten text (or so-called 'foul papers'). Then there is the version that appears in the First Folio (1623) which includes a very large number of small changes, as well as some quite major cuts and additions. The phrase 'hoist with his own petard' (blown up with his own bomb), for example, does not appear in the 1623 text; Hamlet's famous soliloquy at the end of Act 4 scene 4 (beginning 'How all occasions do inform against me') is cut. It is generally supposed that the First Folio text is a revised version of the play based on a scribal transcript (such as a prompt book), and perhaps gives us something closer to the Hamlet

staged in the theatre during Shakespeare's lifetime. But like the
Second Quarto, the 1623 version is still too long to be performed word for word: it is in many respects primarily a
literary text, a text to be read. In the following pages I will
quote from the Oxford edition, which takes the First Folio as
its so-called 'control text'; but I will also emphasize and comment on some of the differences between the Second Quarto
and the 1623 versions.

Just as various phrases from the play have become part of
our everyday speech, so the basic plot of *Hamlet* is perhaps as
well known as any other work in English or indeed world literature. Writers such as Tom Stoppard, in *The Fifteen Minute
Hamlet*, and Richard Curtis, in his altogether more crude
(though also more amusing) *The Skinhead Hamlet*, have sought
to compress the plot; after all, as Polonius says, 'brevity is the
soul of wit' (2.2.90). So, in roughly 175 words: the King of
Denmark, called Hamlet, has been murdered by his brother
Claudius. Claudius marries his brother's wife Gertrude and
becomes the new King. The Ghost of the dead King appears
and tells his son, also called Hamlet (Prince of Denmark),
about the murder. The Prince is grief-stricken at his father's
death and his mother's remarriage. In soliloquy he meditates
on the apparent need to take revenge. He wonders whether
the Ghost is not a devil sent to damn him. He helps stage a
play, 'The Mousetrap', a re-enactment of the alleged murder,
in an attempt to confirm Claudius's culpability. In the end he
does indeed kill Claudius, though with numerous fatal casu-
alties along the way. Hamlet kills Polonius, the father of
Laertes and Ophelia (the young woman who loves Hamlet
and whom Gertrude fondly expects will one day be Hamlet's
wife). Mad with grief at her father's death, Ophelia apparently
drowns herself. Laertes seeks revenge in a duel with Hamlet.

Laertes himself is killed, as is Hamlet. And so, too, is the Queen, a poisoned onlooker.

One of the most striking things about *Hamlet* is the sense that it is as much post-tragedy as tragedy. 'Who's there?' (1.1.1) asks Barnardo, one of the night sentinels, in the opening words of the play, uneasily casting his question into the bitter cold darkness. *Hamlet* begins already in a state of tragic disorder and disturbed mourning, in the wake of the murder of the father, hushed by the terrifying prospect of a return of the dead in the form of his ghost, or rather by *yet another* return. For we quickly gather that the ghost has already appeared, in effect, before the action of the play commences. 'Who's there?' is not simply a question addressed to the living. 'Is that a ghost?' or 'Are you a ghost?' might be another way of putting it. Barnardo's question haunts the play. It hovers restlessly over the final scene, in which Gertrude, Claudius, Laertes and Hamlet die. What is a ghost? What does it mean to 'follow' the dead? Are our words our own? How will our story be told? These are some of the uneasy, troubling questions that arise in the following passage, very close to the end of the play:

HAMLET Here, thou incestuous, murd'rous, damnèd Dane,
Drink off this potion.

He forces Claudius to drink

Is thy union there?
Follow my mother.

Claudius dies

LAERTES   He is justly served;
It is a poison tempered by himself.
Exchange forgiveness with me, noble Hamlet.
Mine and my father's death come not upon thee,
Nor thine on me!   *He dies*

HAMLET   Heaven make thee free of it! I follow thee.
I am dead, Horatio. Wretched Queen, adieu!
You that look pale and tremble at this chance,
That are but mutes or audience to this act,
Had I but time – as this fell sergeant Death
Is strict in his arrest – O, I could tell you –
But let it be. Horatio, I am dead;
Thou liv'st; report me and my cause aright
To the unsatisfied.

HORATIO   Never believe it.
I am more an antique Roman than a Dane.
Here's yet some liquor left.

HAMLET   As thou'rt a man,
Give me the cup. Let go. By heaven, I'll have't.
O God, Horatio, what a wounded name,
Things standing thus unknown, I leave behind me!
If thou didst ever hold me in thy heart,
Absent thee from felicity awhile,
And in this harsh world draw thy breath in pain,
To tell my story.

A march afar off, and shot within

What warlike noise is this?

Enter Osric

OSRIC   Young Fortinbras, with conquest come from Poland,
        To th'ambassadors of England gives
        This warlike volley.
HAMLET   O, I die, Horatio.
        The potent poison quite o'ercrows my spirit.
        I cannot live to hear the news from England,
        But I do prophesy th'election lights
        On Fortinbras. He has my dying voice.
        So tell him, with the occurrents, more and less,
        Which have solicited – the rest is silence.

                He gives a long sigh and dies

HORATIO Now cracks a noble heart. Good night, sweet prince,
        And flights of angels sing thee to thy rest.
        Why does the drum come hither?

                                    (5.2.278–314)

The play has some forty lines still to run, most of them
spoken by Horatio and the newly arrived king-to-be,
Fortinbras. The action immediately preceding the passage has
been fast and furious. There is the duel between Hamlet and
Laertes, a work of treachery, in fact, masterminded by
Claudius. Wishing Hamlet dead, he connives with Laertes to
ensure that the rapier used in the duel against Hamlet is tipped
with a poison mixed or 'tempered' by himself. By way of
back-up, Claudius also arranges for a cup of poisoned wine to
be made available for Hamlet to drink. Laertes's willingness to
connive is based on his grief and outraged family honour following the discovery that Hamlet has killed Laertes's father
Polonius and that his sister Ophelia has herself then gone mad
and drowned. The duel is botched. Hamlet is wounded by

Laertes; the rapiers get mixed up and Hamlet wounds him in turn. Laertes is thus poisoned by his own weapon, 'justly killed with mine own treachery' (5.2.261). The Queen, against the King's advice, drinks from the poisoned cup. ('Fucking odd wine!' is her considered judgement in Curtis's *Skinhead Hamlet*.) Gertrude's final words are notably addressed not to Claudius but to Hamlet: 'O my dear Hamlet! / The drink, the drink! I am poisoned' (5.2.263–4). She dies. The dying Laertes reveals that Hamlet too is dying ('No med'cine in the world can do thee good. / In thee there is not half an hour of life': 5.2.268–9), and that 'the King's to blame' (5.2.274). Hamlet then stabs Claudius and, for good measure, pours some of the poisoned wine into his mouth. This is where the extract starts.

'Here, thou incestuous, murd'rous, damnèd Dane'. The Second Quarto has 'Heare', as in 'Listen to me'. There is some appropriateness in the command to 'Hear', sounding out in the deadly declarative alliteration of 'damnèd Dane, / Drink . . .' 'Here', however, forcefully complements the 'this' of 'this potion': they are examples of deictic language, stressing physical immediacy. The First Folio version also adds a new word, 'murd'rous'. It is a small but crucial addition, since it is the only moment in the entire play when Hamlet actually declares Claudius a murderer to his face, indeed into his very mouth. Likewise Hamlet uses the word 'incestuous' earlier on in soliloquy (1.2.157, 3.3.90), but only now does he confront Claudius with it. In Shakespeare's time, sexual relations between a man and his brother's wife were forbidden by the Protestant and Catholic church alike. As is commanded in the Geneva Bible (first published in 1560 and generally reckoned to be the bible with which Shakespeare would have been most familiar): 'Thou shalt not discover the shame [i.e. nakedness] of thy brother's wife: for it is thy brother's shame' (Leviticus 18.16). Hamlet's 'incestuous, murd'rous, damnèd' also aptly recalls the Ghost's original revelation of the murder at the end of Act 1: the words 'murder', 'incestuous' and indeed 'damnèd incest' were all initially spoken by the Ghost (1.5.25, 42, 83). In the next line the First Folio changes the Second Quarto's 'of' ('Drink of this potion') to the more physically expressive and final 'off'. The stage direction '*He forces Claudius to drink*' (in the Oxford edition) is in fact in neither the Second Quarto nor the First Folio, even if its sense seems clearly implied in both.

Hamlet plays on words to the last, above all in asking the magnificent rhetorical question, 'Is thy union there?' A little earlier Claudius has himself used this word 'union', referring to a splendid pearl, dropped into the wine: he says he will drink to Hamlet's 'better breath' or enhanced stamina in the duel, 'And in the cup an union shall he [Claudius] throw / Richer than that which four successive kings / In Denmark's crown have worn' (5.2.218–21). The Second Quarto fails to make this richly loaded joke at all: there we read 'the Onixe', not 'thy union'. Hamlet's question in the 1623 version refers to 'union' also in the sense of marriage, and the prospect of the King's being united with Gertrude in death. 'Is thy union there? / Follow my mother.' 'Follow' looks simple enough, yet is one of the most enigmatic words in the entire play. Here it is a strange instance of the imperative: is it an order ('I order you to follow') or request ('Please follow'), or the expression of a desire, a prayer, a hope, or indeed a fear? The last words that Claudius ever hears are 'Follow my mother'; but follow her *where*? Hamlet evidently regards Claudius as 'damnèd', but it is not clear that he supposes a 'union' taking place in hell. Besides numerous instances of 'follow[ing]' other characters, and even of following a corpse – in the form of

Ophelia's coffin (5.1.210) – 'follow' is a key word in *Hamlet* in relation to the Ghost. When the Ghost of his father appears in Act 1 scene 4, Hamlet repeatedly says that he will follow (1.4.43, 47, 54, 61). What does it mean to follow a ghost? This is not simply a question about going after, but also of obedience and inheritance, of listening to and understanding the dead. The motif of 'following' in *Hamlet* is, perhaps inevitably, ghostly, and strangely fails to follow: it constitutes a kind of terrifying non sequitur. Apparently logical and straightforward, it repeatedly leads to the sense of a sort of mad precipice, like 'the dreadful summit of the cliff / That beetles o'er his base into the sea' (1.4.49–50) about which Horatio warns Hamlet when he first vows to 'follow' the Ghost in Act 1.

With his last words Laertes seeks to '[e]xchange forgiveness' with Hamlet: 'Mine and my father's death come not upon thee, / Nor thine on me!' (5.2.282–4). The inadvertent exchange of rapiers is now to be exchanged for the heartfelt exchange of forgiveness. Hamlet blesses Laertes: 'Heaven make thee free of it! I follow thee.' Here is 'follow' again, noticeably close on the heels of 'Follow my mother.' Does Hamlet mean to suggest that he 'follow[s]' Laertes to heaven, as Horatio's brief verbal requiem about the singing of 'flights of angels' might appear to corroborate? Or does he just mean to say 'I am a goner as well'? *Hamlet* sends mixed messages on the question of where you go once you have 'shuffled off this mortal coil' (3.1.68): purgatory, heaven and hell are all proffered, along with the apparent capacity, once having shuffled off, to shuffle back again. (*Enter the Ghost.*) But above all as an effect of this very mixture, Shakespeare's play exacerbates a sense of the unknown, a sense of puzzle and dread at the thought of death as 'The undiscovered country, from whose bourn ['boundary' or 'frontier'] / No traveller returns' (3.1.80–1).

'I am dead, Horatio', says Hamlet. He is not quite dead yet, but realizes he is dying, and can scarcely speak. Shakespeare is here, as usual, doing strange things with words. 'Wretched Queen, adieu!' This address or apostrophe is in some ways as bizarre as saying 'I am dead', for the Queen of course is herself already dead. But then again *Hamlet* is also, from start to finish, a play that renders uncertain all assumptions about who is dead and who is not. 'Wretched' has the sense of 'unhappy' but also 'pitiable': it is a loving if agonized valedictory adjective. But the 'adieu' poignantly, if also rather eerily, recalls the Ghost once more. It is the Ghost's word in Act 1 scene 5: 'Adieu, adieu, Hamlet. Remember me' (1.5.91). It seems that the son does remember. It is as if the Ghost comes back again, speaking through the son, to say 'adieu' to his former wife. The 'adieu' is a kind of double-voicing, uncertainly living and dead. 'You that look pale and tremble at his chance, / That are but mutes or audience to this act, / Had I but time . . .' Hamlet stumbles, his words are arrested, split off into aposiopesis, the rhetorical figure for an unfinished statement. 'Had I but time . . . O, I could tell you – / But let it be.' These lines constitute one of the most remarkable instances of metatheatrical address anywhere in Shakespeare's work. Hamlet's words are explicitly *about* the fact that they are theatrical, that they are words being spoken on the stage.

There are of course many examples of metatheatricality in Shakespeare. We may think of 'Pyramus and Thisbe', the play-within-the-play in Act 5 of *A Midsummer Night's Dream*; Cassius's extraordinary celebration of the assassination of Caesar: 'How many ages hence / Shall this our lofty scene be acted over / In states unborn and accents yet unknown!' (*Julius Caesar* 3.1.111–3); Jaques's 'All the world's a stage' and Rosalind's epilogue to the audience in *As You Like It*; or the

pageant of Prospero's 'revels' (4.1.148) in *The Tempest*.
Hamlet's words are in some respects understated by comparison, and yet all the more insidious and haunting in effect. First
of all it is perhaps not immediately obvious to whom Hamlet's
words *are* addressed. Evidently turning from the dead Queen,
he says: 'You that look pale and tremble at this chance, / That
are but mutes or audience to this act . . .' 'Chance' here has the
sense of 'unexpected event' or, more ironically, 'mischance'.
The 'you' on the other hand would appear first of all to mean
those who are present on stage but who do not speak. Mutes
are speechless actors. It is as if the daring of Hamlet's use of
the word 'mutes' immediately calls for a toning down, for the
qualification of an 'or' ('or audience'). And yet this very alter-
nation or tempering enhances the poisonous effect: the 'or'
can also be read as 'and'; it is not possible to hear or read
Hamlet's words as addressed merely to those ostensibly on
stage. These words are directed beyond the stage, addressing
us, as readers or spectators. The double meaning of 'act'
accentuates this, playing with and across distinctions between
the theatrical and non-theatrical, between what is on and
what is off stage. It recalls and reactivates earlier appearances in
the play, for example, 'act' as 'effect' (1.2.205), as 'event'
(1.5.84), as 'deed' (3.4.41), and as 'theatrical scene' (3.2.73).
The 'you' becomes us, transmuted, the speechless audience,
readers who are 'but mutes'. In its plural form as a noun,
'mutes' features in no other speech in Shakespeare's plays.
The only other occasion on which it occurs in *Hamlet*, and
then only in the First Folio version, is itself mute: it appears in
the stage directions for the performance of the dumb show.
The Queen leaves the King asleep on '*a bank of flowers . . .
Anon comes in a fellow, takes off his crown, kisses it, and pours
poison in the King's ears, and exits. The Queen returns, finds the*

King dead, and makes passionate action. The Poisoner, with some two or three Mutes, comes in again, seeming to lament with her' (stage directions at 3.2.126). Our final role as silent onlookers ('mutes or audience') is here eerily inscribed at the heart of the work, in the dumb show (or, if you will, the mute show) before the play-within-the-play.

There is something else strange about these words, 'You that look pale and tremble at this chance'. It has to do with what I described in the chapter on *The Merchant of Venice* as examples of thought transference or mental contagion of words, whereby one character unknowingly repeats something said by another. It is the literally *angelic* structure of language (words as strange messengers in flight) that we noted in *Julius Caesar*, whereby the word 'angel' strangely communicates between Antony and Brutus, without either being aware of the fact. Hamlet's address raises questions of telepathy or thought citation in Shakespeare, for which there seems as yet to be little developed critical vocabulary. The words 'You that look pale and tremble' convey a strange sense of magical thinking. Hamlet's phrasing recalls a moment very close to the beginning of the play, when he himself was not present on stage. In the opening scene, just after midnight, Horatio joins other guards on the watch. Marcellus and Barnardo claim to have seen a ghost on two occasions, including the previous night. Horatio is sceptical: he thinks it is 'but [their] fantasy' (1.1.23), in other words merely their deluded imagination. Then the Ghost appears. Horatio, in a state of 'fear and wonder', charges it to speak, but 'it stalks away' (1.1.44, 50). Following the Ghost's exit Barnardo exclaims: 'How now, Horatio? You tremble and look pale. / Is not this something more than fantasy?' (1.1.53–4). When Hamlet later speaks his dying words, 'You that look pale and tremble', there is a strange enactment or re-enactment. Horatio, and we as mutes or audience, have heard these words before.

Hamlet flounders around failing to finish his sentences. How are we to follow him? He no longer has time to 'report' his 'cause aright' or tell his story. No Shakespeare play has more obvious topicality or urgency in terms of thinking about nuclear war (what used to be called 'mutual assured destruction' or MAD), the deadly logic of revenge calling forth revenge (the Middle East, the war on terror), or the terrible ironies of 'success' at the cost of losing one's own life (the suicide bomber). More than any other character in Shakespeare, Hamlet gives us the sense of someone who has looked into the very depths of what it is to be 'human', who has grasped terrible truths and cannot survive what he has experienced. Hamlet is not real, and yet this fictional creation bizarrely manages to leave us wondering what more he would have said, as well as how to respond to what we have witnessed.

Hamlet's closest friend, Horatio, responds by making to kill himself, in the manner of 'an antique Roman' (like Brutus in *Julius Caesar*, or Antony in *Antony and Cleopatra*). Hamlet's outrage at this suggests that there are two things more important than life itself: the story and the name. 'O God, Horatio, what a wounded name, / Things standing thus unknown, I leave behind me!' We have already encountered the crucial importance of the name. Earlier on in Act 5 scene 2, Laertes says that it is only in 'terms of honour' (not 'in nature' or in terms of his feelings) that he is compelled to fight Hamlet: it is necessary, he says, in order '[t]o keep my name ungored' (5.2.192, 196). Likewise in a brief passage that appears in the Second Quarto but is omitted from the First Folio, Claudius expresses to Gertrude his hope that the 'poisoned' cannon shot of telltale 'whisper' (in particular regarding the death of Polonius) 'may miss our name / And hit the woundless air' (3.4.41–4). In this context it is difficult not to think also of the fact that the name of Shakespeare's only son was Hamnet (a variant form of 'Hamlet'): he was born in 1585 and died in 1596. Shakespeare's own name and story, his legacy and we must suppose also his grief and mourning, are thus inscribed in this play, starting from the very title. For Hamlet, the only way of keeping a name unwounded is to be able to 'tell [the] story' of its bearer, to 'report . . . aright' what the dying person has done and why.

Other events of national and international significance are happening around Hamlet. Fortinbras arrives from Poland and Hamlet gives him his support (his 'dying voice') as the next King of Denmark; and there is also 'news from England'. All of this is punctuated by strange sounds suggestive of further trouble ('warlike noise', 'warlike volley', the beatings of the military 'drum'). Hamlet's ultimate and presiding concern, however, is with ensuring that Fortinbras is acquainted with everything that has happened, 'with the occurrents, more and less, / Which have solicited – the rest is silence.' Despite the First Folio having a full stop after 'solicited' ('moved', 'brought forth', 'urged'), most editions insert a dash, in order to stress the sense that this is another aposiopesis or unfinished sentence. Tell Fortinbras all the occurrences that moved (me to act as I did), urged (me to give him my support). 'The rest is silence' interrupts as well as concludes the sentence and sense.

'If thou didst ever hold me in thy heart . . .' It is absolutely crucial to the ending of the play that Hamlet's closest friend Horatio live on. Without Horatio, we realize, there would be no one to tell the story as we have understood it. But what is 'the story'? Is Horatio's story of 'the occurrents' the same as the one we would recount? Amid a scene of carnage that is 'dismal' (5.2.320) and where 'men's minds are wild' (5.2.347), Horatio goes on to promise to tell 'to th' yet unknowing world / How these things came about' (5.2.332–3). But perhaps the most astonishing effect of the ending of Shakespeare's play consists in a sense of strangely stopping short, of something terribly foreclosed, of a tale still to be unfolded. There is something like an aposiopesis of thinking and feeling. We are solicited. The rest is up to us, mutes.

5

SEEL

Othello

What are you seeing in front of your eyes, on the page or stage? *Othello* is in some respects the most simple, even blindingly obvious of Shakespeare's so-called 'great tragedies'. In comparison with *Hamlet*, *King Lear* and *Macbeth*, it may seem quite pared down. Iago, the nastiest piece of work anywhere in Shakespeare, manages to talk his master, the 'noble Moor' Othello, into believing that Othello's lovely young wife Desdemona has been having sex with another man, Cassio, and gets Othello to murder her (and then kill himself). No other Shakespeare tragedy depends so much on what one man can do to another through the sheer power and cunning of his language. (Iago is also somewhat aided by luck, in particular by managing to acquire a handkerchief that had been Othello's 'first gift' to Desdemona, which he lies to Othello about having '[seen] Cassio wipe his beard with' (3.3.439–42). He plants it in Cassio's lodging, thus fabricating what looks like firm evidence for the credibility of his story regarding Desdemona's infidelity.) Nowhere else in

Shakespeare are we so exposed to witnessing the terrible, deadly consequences of one man persuading another to see and act upon what is not real. In persuading Othello to regard his wife as a 'lewd minx' (3.3.478), a lascivious, worthless slut who has, with Othello's own trusted lieutenant Cassio, 'the act of shame / A thousand times committed' (5.2.209–10), Iago can seem almost magical, a kind of genius, a figure of the devilishly creative artist or director at work within the play. But to see what is not there, as I hope to make clear, is also a sort of blindness, a blindness to seeing what *is* there. I will explore this idea, towards the end of the chapter, through a focus on the word 'seel'. To seel is to blind, to blindfold or hoodwink or, more literally, to sew up the eyelids. The word originally related to the practice of sewing up the eyelids of a young falcon as a means to training it.

The earliest known reference to *Othello* is to the performance of a play called 'The Moor of Venis' at the Banqueting House, in Whitehall, London, on 1 November 1604. Generally thought to have been written in 1603–4, *Othello* was first published in a quarto in 1622 and then the following year in the First Folio. Both the Quarto and Folio editions are reckoned to be 'good', 'authoritative' texts. There are, however, striking differences: the Folio has approximately 160 extra lines; there are more than a thousand variations in vocabulary; and the Quarto contains some 53 oaths not found in the Folio version. Editors usually come up with a version of the play that is based on the First Folio but that also makes use of many details, including the oaths, found only in the Quarto. How we read *Othello*, then, can be intimately affected by these differences, and I will mention at least a couple in the reading that follows.

Othello is a play about the mad and deathly power of

jealousy; seeing and blindness; the visibility and significance of 'blackness', racial and ethnic difference; religion and war (Christianity vs. Islam, Venetians vs. Turks); storytelling and witchcraft. Set in Venice and Cyprus, in around 1570–71, the play focuses on the military hero Othello who is called upon to defend Cyprus (an outpost of Christian Europe then belonging to the Venetian Republic) from the attacking Turks. It is not clear from Shakespeare's play how dark-skinned Othello is supposed to be. This ambiguity means that he can be played as a black African, or as a 'tawny' Moor like the Prince of Morocco in *The Merchant of Venice* (2.1.1, s.d.). There is no doubt, however, that racism is a fundamental issue in the play: 'blackness' is repeatedly associated with what is devilish, and from the opening scene Othello is evoked as a 'gross' and 'lascivious' figure (1.1.124). Iago draws together associations of devilry and bestial sexuality when he awakens Desdemona's father Brabantio with the words: 'Even now, now, very now, an old black ram [Othello] / Is tupping [shagging] your white ewe [Desdemona]. Arise, arise, / . . . / Or else the devil will make a grandsire of you' (1.1.87–90). The superstitious Brabantio is convinced that Othello has used 'foul charms' and bound his daughter in 'chains of magic' (1.2.73, 65). By his own account, however, the only 'witch-craft' (1.3.170) Othello has used is in telling Desdemona 'the story of my life / From year to year – the battles, sieges, for-tunes / That I have passed' (1.3.130–32). Othello's black-ness, his sexuality and his military prowess remain key aspects of the play; but the bigger picture of Christianity and Islam at war quickly fades. Thanks to a storm that wreaks havoc on the Turkish fleet, the threat to Cyprus has disappeared by the beginning of Act 2: 'Our wars are done' (2.1.20), as an un-named Venetian gentleman summarily puts it.

The rest of the play unfolds in a strangely interior and inward fashion, above all thanks to the ways in which Shakespeare exposes and explores the murderous workings of Iago's mind. We know from a soliloquy at the end of Act 1 that Iago 'hate[s] the Moor' (1.3.367, 385), suspecting him (for no obvious or substantiated reason) of having had sex with his own wife, Emilia. And we know that he sees Othello as a gullible man, who 'thinks men honest that but seem to be so' and who can therefore be 'led by the nose' as 'tenderly' or easily as an ass (1.3.399–401). The form of the soliloquy is crucial: it is a kind of materialization of what is nowadays called 'magical thinking'. As readers or spectators we are made a party to the character's inner thoughts and feelings. The soliloquy allows us horrible insight into Iago's own devilish cogitations and desires. Although Iago remains a profoundly disturbing and enigmatic character to the very end of the play, we are given a remarkable inner knowledge of how his mind works. Shakespeare deploys a range of visual metaphors and other turns of phrase, in this context, to foreground the strange but compelling idea of 'thought' itself being visible. His language encourages us to imagine that we can effectively 'see' Iago's inner thought processes and share in the moment of their unfolding. Here, as in so many other places in Shakespeare's plays, we are invited into a kind of magical or telepathic space. 'Let me see now . . . Let's see' (1.3.391, 393), Iago says in the early soliloquy, and then announces the sudden discovery: 'I have't. It is engendered. Hell and night / Must bring this monstrous birth to the world's light' (1.3.402–3). His plan is monstrous, and through this strange exposure of inner thoughts and feelings that we name 'soliloquy' we become witnesses. Shakespeare plays on the putative etymological link between 'monster' and the Latin verb *monstrare*, 'to show'. For the monstrous offspring of Iago's weird mental coitus we must wait; but we have in effect already been drawn into his mind, exposed to a place in which thinking can be monstrously shown.

Let us pursue these issues by turning to Act 3 scene 3, sometimes known as the 'temptation scene'. Regarded by many (including me and the Arden editor E. A. J. Honigmann) as the single most extraordinary scene in all of Shakespeare's plays, it begins with Othello unquestioningly in love with his wife Desdemona and ends with his vowing to seek 'some swift means of death / For the fair devil' (3.3.480–81). In the course of this scene, Othello's mind, his very sense of himself and of his life or 'occupation' (3.3.360), is transformed by Iago's devastating words. Everything in this play depends on the strange idea of knowing, or thinking one can know, someone else's thoughts, of thinking that one can see thought, see what is not an object of vision. 'Thought' is the word that Iago drops into the conversation early on in Act 3 scene 3. Just wondering – just 'for a satisfaction of my thought' (3.3.97) – he asks Othello how much his lieutenant Cassio knew about Othello's love for Desdemona when Othello was wooing her. Iago needs to arouse Othello's suspicion regarding Cassio's relationship with her. Othello asks, 'Is [Cassio] not honest?' (3.3.103). Did you say 'honest', my lord? Sort of, I guess, 'My lord, for aught I know' (3.3.106), Iago replies.

Iago tinkers with thought. When Othello then asks in some exasperation, 'What dost thou think?', Iago merely turns the word back on him: 'Think, my lord?' (3.3.107–8). Othello's anger at this point is underscored by his switch to the third person ('he') to refer to the person to whom he is speaking. It is as if Iago (or implicitly Othello likewise) is beside himself, already an echo of himself: 'Think, my lord! By heaven, he echoes me, / As if there were some monster in his [Iago's] thought / Too hideous to be shown' (3.3.109–11). ('He echoes' and 'his' here are the 1622 version: in 1623 we find the less distinctive, less strange and out of place 'thou echo'st' and 'thy'.) We might indeed think of the entire play as an enormous, eerie echo chamber. The overall impression is that Iago works 'by wit [cleverness, quickness of judgement] and not by witchcraft' (2.3.367); yet the play is pervaded by references to magic and by a sense of the telepathic or nearly telepathic.

At the heart of the plot is the handkerchief that Othello gives Desdemona and that Iago makes Othello think she has given in turn to Cassio. As Othello tells her in Act 3 scene 4, this handkerchief was originally given to his mother by an Egyptian 'charmer' who 'could almost read / The thoughts of people' (3.4.53–4). The idea of thought reading or thought transmission is a striking dimension of Shakespeare's play. It is as if some telepathic transfer were going on in Act 3 scene 3, for example, when Iago's 'monstrous birth' (1.3.403) is weirdly echoed or reiterated in Othello's 'monster in his thought'. Iago plays with pauses, breakings off or 'stops' (3.3.123) in his speech. At once provoking and holding back, he teases Othello: 'It were not for your quiet nor your good / Nor for my manhood, honesty and wisdom / To let you know my thoughts' (3.3.155–7). Othello then explodes with: 'Zounds! [i.e. By Christ's wounds!] What dost thou mean?' (3.3.157). This 'Zounds!' is one of the 53 oaths omitted from the First Folio. It is generally supposed that such omissions were part of an attempt to comply with the Act of Abuses (1606) which made it unlawful to use profane language on stage. Some modern editors prefer 'Zounds!', some 'What dost thou mean?'; others go for both. In any case, the profane reference to Christ's wounds is, at this point, characteristic of Iago rather than Othello: 'Zounds' is used twice by Iago, for example, in the opening scene of the play (1.1.85 and 107). Othello's use of it here is another instance of the strange Shakespeared echo chamber.

It is better to be a cuckold who 'lives in bliss' and doesn't care about 'his wronger' (his wife) (3.3.169–70). There is nothing worse, Iago suggests, than being someone who 'dotes yet doubts, suspects yet strongly loves' (3.3.169, 172). Iago's play on 'dote' and 'doubt' seems to inspire Othello to indulge in a sort of wordplay in turn. 'Think'st thou I'd make a life of jealousy?', he asks. 'No: to be once in doubt / Is once to be resolved' (3.3.180, 182–3). He tries to dismiss doubt, in other words, on the basis of the idea that to be in doubt is once and for all to have made one's mind up. It is to have things 'resolved' – as if, paradoxically, no longer in doubt. This is how the exchange then develops:

OTHELLO   No, Iago,
            I'll see before I doubt, when I doubt, prove,
            And on the proof there is no more but this:
            Away at once with love or jealousy!
IAGO   I am glad of this, for now I shall have reason
            To show the love and duty that I bear you
            With franker spirit: therefore, as I am bound,
            Receive it from me. I speak not yet of proof:
            Look to your wife, observe her well with Cassio.
            Wear your eyes thus, not jealous nor secure;
            I would not have your free and noble nature
            Out of self-bounty be abused: look to't.
            I know our country disposition well –

> In Venice they do let God see the pranks
> They dare not show their husbands; their best conscience
> Is not to leave't undone, but keep't unknown.

OTHELLO   Dost thou say so?

IAGO   She did deceive her father, marrying you,
> And when she seemed to shake, and fear your looks,
> She loved them most.

OTHELLO   And so she did.

IAGO   Why, go to then:
> She that so young could give out such a seeming
> To seel her father's eyes up, close as oak –
> He thought 'twas witchcraft. But I am much to blame,
> I humbly do beseech you of your pardon
> For too much loving you.

OTHELLO   I am bound to thee for ever.

IAGO   I see this hath a little dashed your spirits.

OTHELLO   Not a jot, not a jot.

IAGO   I'faith, I fear it has.
> I hope you will consider what is spoke
> Comes from my love. But I do see you're moved . . .

                                                     (3.3.192–221)

We are only halfway through the so-called 'temptation scene', but already Othello is thinking in terms of dramatic resolution: he *will* see. Seeing comes before doubting. Once he doubts (but he must, of course, already have begun to doubt), he only requires proof and then (in stage performance Othello at this point could be expected to produce a suggestively violent gesture with his arm), 'Away at once with love or jealousy!' A sense of finality in the word 'once' has rather ominously imposed itself: 'to be once in doubt / Is once to be resolved', 'Away at once'. Earlier in this book, I remarked on the wordplay on 'Moor' and 'more' in *The Merchant of Venice*. Othello is not a character with whom one associates wordplay: this is generally seen to be Iago's dubious privilege. As elsewhere in Shakespeare, however, it is a question of conceiving wordplay in ways that go beyond mere wit, triviality, punning or quibbling, and indeed that go beyond considerations of what is or is not 'in character'. As noted in 'Witsnapper', there are, literally, no 'puns' or 'quibbles' in Shakespeare: these terms do not appear. Nor is it necessarily a question of what the character Othello *intends*. Indeed, the whole notion of intention seems odd in the context of Othello: he reacts, constantly, to others and to situations, but he does not plan. Rather it is a question of how language itself strangely echoes and enmeshes, doubles and displaces. In Othello's peremptorily resolving that it is all a matter of reacting to 'the proof', we might then also pick up the hint that 'there is no [Moor] but this', i.e. everything is to rest on this, and it will prove to be the end of him. Wordplay in Shakespeare is not opposed to seriousness. On the contrary, it can kill. It can be at once funny and grave, hilarious and terrible.

The dialogue between Othello and Iago in Act 3 scene 3 is perhaps the most disquieting in Shakespeare: in the apparently spontaneous, improvised form of shared discourse, one man's cunning words destroy another's world, shatter the very basis of his interlocutor's identity or 'occupation'. It brings to mind a dictum formulated by Elizabeth Bowen in a quite different context, vis-à-vis the art of writing dialogue in a novel: 'Dialogue must appear realistic without being so.'[6] It is difficult to suppose that anyone could dream and scheme as fast and surely as Iago in this passage: it is a further illustration of what I have been calling Shakespeared language.

'I am glad of this; for now I shall have reason / To show the love and duty that I bear you / With franker spirit': as always, there is as much going on in the little words as in the bigger ones. The introduction of 'reason' is significant: an apparent counter to 'doubt', it links with and elaborates on the importance of 'proof'. Iago has indeed already taken up the language of argument and demonstration with the word 'for' ('for now I shall have reason'). More cunning, however, is the projection into the future, the deployment of the word 'shall'. He might have said 'for now I have reason'; but that is not Iago's way. He subtly holds forth ('now') and withholds ('shall').

He speaks the language of 'reason' but also of vision: everything in this passage is articulated in terms of the strange motif of thinking and visibility noted earlier. There is an apparent promise or commitment to make visible. The apparent intention to 'show . . . love and duty' recalls and ostensibly (but in horribly ironic mode) reverses Othello's image of 'some monster . . . / Too hideous to be shown' (3.3.110–11). Iago insidiously mingles 'spirit' and sight: 'To show . . . / With franker spirit'. A little later in the passage he will reinvoke this link between seeing and spirit (or spirits) to especially devastating effect: 'I see this hath a little dashed your spirits.' 'Franker' is, frankly, a sort of Iago innovation. With its sense of 'more free and open', 'less reserved', 'franker' participates in a kind of double- or Janus-headed wordplay. In one direction it is part of a complex engagement with the question of what is 'free' as regards issues of slavery, servitude, being 'bound', and what Iago consistently refers to as Othello's 'free and open nature' (1.3.398). (The word 'frank' derives from the Latin *francus*, 'free'.) In another direction 'franker' connects with the scene's underdrift towards greater sexual explicitness, towards becoming 'franker' both in speech and in terms of the sexual acts described. By the end of Act 3 scene 3 Iago will be talking about the voyeuristic fantasy of Desdemona being 'topped', i.e. fucked, by Cassio, while Othello 'grossly gape[s] on' (3.3.398–9). But even without these complex resonances, 'franker' is an odd word. It is the only occasion on which this comparative adjective appears in Shakespeare. It is peculiarly apt for Iago: frankness is not straightforward, there are different degrees; showing one's love with 'franker spirit' suggests, once again, a holding forth and a withholding ('franker' but not completely 'frank'). I might be completely frank soon, but not yet, and even then . . . Elsewhere in Shakespeare's play 'frank' is just plain 'frank' (as in 1.3.39).

'Therefore,' Iago goes on, in the language of reason and logical demonstration, 'as I am bound, / Receive it from me.' One of the surreptitious beauties of this sentence is the word 'it' – as if it is already evident what it is. Another is the word 'Receive', which suggests ease and purity of communication but is also an imperative; it is the first time, in fact, that Iago gives Othello an order. The roles of master and servant are reversed. The clause 'as I am bound' appears to qualify the reversal (I am bound to you as your ancient, and bound to 'show' you my 'love and duty'). But Iago has, only a couple of minutes earlier, released 'bound' into the conversation in a decidedly duplicitous way. At that point he suggested that to 'utter [his] thoughts' would go beyond even slavery: 'Good my lord, pardon me; / Though I am bound to every act of duty / I am not bound to that all slaves are free to' (3.3.136–8). Even slaves are free to think. 'Therefore, as I am bound' – but not really bound, because I am still not uttering my thoughts . . .

Paralipsis is the name for the rhetorical figure whereby someone says something by pretending not to say it. A familiar example might be 'I shall not speak of his generosity'. Here is another, decidedly cunning version of it: 'I speak not yet of proof.' Iago speaks of 'proof', and surreptitiously construes that as proof of guilt, not proof of guilt *or* innocence, even as he speaks of not (yet) doing so. And then comes a stream of urgings, all relating to the visual: 'Look to your wife', 'observe her well with Cassio', 'Wear your eyes thus', 'look to't'. These are not quite or not only imperatives, but rather of the meddling genre: '(I would strongly advise you to) do this', 'do that'. Here is one of the most disturbing lines in this tragedy: 'Wear your eyes thus, not jealous nor secure.' Try doing this at home: it's not so simple. There is something terrible but also perhaps horribly funny about it. Indeed, this is one of the moments in the play where we may feel how much closer to comedy *Othello* is than any other Shakespeare tragedy. The intimate and specific nature of his advice indicates how confident the subordinate Iago has now grown in terms of what he feels able to say to his master and get away with. One tiny difference between the 1622 and 1623 versions emphasizes the bizarre suggestion. The Quarto has the more figurative 'eye' in the singular; the Folio's plural 'eyes' is more literal and physical. To 'wear [one's] eyes' is a strange image, already suggestive of the eyes as somehow additional or supplementary, like articles of clothing, a crown or flower or beard. How or where do you look, when someone tells you to 'wear your eyes' negatively, neither in this way nor in that? There is perhaps a hint of an unfathomable homophone ('where?') in Iago's 'wear'. Look like this, like me now, but at the same time not me; be yourself, 'free and noble'. Iago seems set on tying Othello's eyes in nots: 'not jealous nor secure'; not jealous, not free from care; not suspicious, not unsuspicious. It is not entirely surprising, perhaps, that Othello will shortly be having an epileptic fit or two (see 4.1.50–51). Iago is sending Othello crazy, turning him into a jealousy-deranged killer before our very eyes.

Iago's shift to the mock-caring conditional 'I would not' (I should not wish anyone to abuse your free and noble nature) is apparently futural but also twists itself in a sadistic present. The reader or spectator is sharply aware that, in the very act of saying 'I would not have your free and noble nature / Out of self-bounty be abused', Iago is abusing Othello. 'Self-bounty' is a neologism, Shakespeared language for '(your) own goodness', 'innate generosity': Iago is ironically attributing to Othello a capacity for freedom and kindness that he will never have again. He plays on Othello's lack of social confidence but also on his foreignness. Iago can speak of 'our country' in the sense of *his* but not Othello's. 'I know our country disposition well – / In Venice they do let God see the pranks / They dare not show their husbands.' Here is the sexually 'franker' mode. Celebrated in the sixteenth century for its courtesans and sexual licentiousness, Venice is the place where 'they' – Iago leaves it suggestively unspecific, neither 'wives' nor 'women', a truly promiscuous 'they' – get up to all sorts of sexual antics. They do stuff they would never 'show their husbands', but they don't care if God sees. In fact that might be part of the attraction. Their highest sense of morality ('best conscience') is to not let it be known about. In these three or four lines Iago extends the domain of the visual in remarkable ways. The 1623 Folio has 'heaven' instead of 'God': the Quarto version is more powerful and shocking. There is the provocative suggestion of God watching sex, looking at sexual acts,

or rather being allowed to look ('let God see'). At the same
time, recalling and reworking the verb 'to show' (a 'monster . . .
/ Too hideous to be shown', 'to show the love and duty that I
bear you'), Iago evokes what is concealed from husbands. We
are left to suppose, then, that Iago himself sees, or at least
knows. If only implicitly, he takes up a Godlike position of his
own. There is also of course a dabbling here with 'cunt', in
'country disposition' and 'best countenance'. Othello may not
be expected to pick up the more bawdy resonances, but he
needs to appear at least a little shocked: 'Dost thou say so?'

'Dost thou say so?' This stupid non-question allows Iago to
move on and deliver the killer lines: 'She did deceive her
father, marrying you, / And when she seemed to shake, and
fear your looks, / She loved them most.' Iago is recalling the
fact that Desdemona kept her love for Othello, and indeed her
marriage to him, secret from her father. He is also recalling
particular phrases from Brabantio, ghostly words coming back
now to produce new and deadly effects. In particular, Iago is
here reworking Brabantio's expression of incredulity that his
daughter should have been able '[t]o fall in love with what she
feared to look on' (1.3.99). Desdemona was 'love-shaked'
with a difference, seduced by fear, loving Othello most when
he looked most scary. There is a sort of double deception
implied: Desdemona deceived her father, but there was also
something deceptive about the manner in which she loved
Othello. (We might additionally note here that Iago has devi-
ously, almost imperceptibly, slipped Desdemona's love for
Othello into the past tense.) There is perhaps a further thread
in Iago's words, an unspoken encouragement: don't be afraid
of making her fear you, she loves it really. But in these lines
Iago is also recalling and revising Brabantio's last words to
Othello, near the end of Act 1: 'Look to her, Moor, if thou

hast eyes to see: / She has deceived her father, and may thee'
(1.3.293–4). Intriguingly, Iago retains Brabantio's reference
to looking ('Look to her', 'fear your looks'), but appears to
suppress or elide the question of Othello's 'eyes' ('if thou hast
eyes to see').

   This, perhaps, is the very moment of blinding. 'And so she
did,' acknowledges Othello. 'Why, go to then,' says Iago, there
you are, what did I tell you. 'She that so young could give out
such a seeming / To seel her father's eyes up, close as oak – /
He thought 'twas witchcraft . . .' As I noted at the start of this
chapter, 'to seel' means to blind or, more specifically, to sew
up the eyelids. It is perhaps difficult not to read 'seel' here as
a homophone for 'seal' as well. The 1623 Folio, indeed, spells
the word 'seale'; and the metaphor 'close as oak', suggestive of
the knotted, close grain of that wood, works at least as well for
'seal' as 'seel'. Everything, in a sense, seems to be seeled and
sealed up at this point. Strange things have been going on in
the sibilants in this passage. The sounds of the 'see' ('I'll see
before I doubt', 'let God see', 'receive', 'deceive') pass through
'seem' ('she seemed to shake', 'such a seeming'), coming to a
stop in 'seel'. There is also a strange effect gathering in the
repetition of the word 'so' ('Dost thou say so?', 'And so she
did', 'so young'), as if the 'seel' has suggested itself through a
connection with the homophone 'sew'. Shakespeare plays
elsewhere on 'so' and 'sew' (see, for example, *The Two
Gentlemen of Verona*, 3.1.297–8); and of course sewing is significant in the following scene of *Othello* when Othello
describes how his mother on her deathbed asked him to give
the handkerchief to the woman he married. 'I did so,' he tells
Desdemona, and then goes on to record that '[a] sibyl . . .
sewed the work [i.e. the embroidery]' on the handkerchief, in
'prophetic fury' (3.4.67–74).

'Seel' here is not simply Iago's word, in any case. It is an ironic echoing and strange displacement of something Othello says near the end of Act 1. There he scoffs at the thought of a time 'when light-winged toys / Of feathered Cupid seel with wanton dullness / My speculative and officed instrument' (1.3.269–71), i.e. when the caresses and dallyings of love blind with amorous sleepiness my capacity for clear vision in my duties. It is as if, with this word, Othello seels his own fate. 'She that so young could give out such a seeming / To seel her father's eyes up, close as oak – / He thought 'twas witchcraft . . .' And then Iago stops, cuts the thread, apologizing on account of supposedly loving his master 'too much'. The reversal and the stitch-up are accomplished. Othello is 'bound to [Iago] for ever'. Later in Act 3 scene 3 we encounter the handkerchief, the '[trifle] light as air' (3.3.322) that Iago will use as 'ocular proof' (3.3.363) of Cassio's intimacy with Desdemona; but the most decisive ocular proof is here and now, on the stage or page, in witnessing Othello's being visibly moved: 'I see this hath a little dashed your spirits.' Othello tries in vain to deny it ('Not a jot', not a bit, he says); Iago reaffirms: 'But I do see you're moved' (3.3.221).

Act 3 scene 3 of *Othello* is perhaps not so much the 'temptation scene' as the 'seeling scene'. If Act 3 scene 3 seels Othello's fate, it also figures as a kind of seal for the tragedy as a whole. In the closing scene Othello murders his innocent wife; Iago murders his own wife, Emilia; and finally Othello kills himself. Iago the devilish engineer of the entire show now vows to say nothing: 'Demand me nothing. What you know, you know' (5.2.300). And so: what does anyone learn in the end? Iago is to be tortured, but we are never to discover its outcome. In the grim final lines of the play the Venetian gentleman Ludovico gestures towards the bed where the dead

Desdemona and Othello lie and simply says: 'This object [i.e. this spectacle, this object of vision] poisons sight, / Let it be hid' (5.2.362–3). If, to recall Iago's phrasing, the play is about 'bring[ing a] monstrous birth to the world's light' (1.3.403), the final impulse is to conceal it again, indeed to hide it. The spectacle is poisonous to the eye, as if blinding. It is better to be blind to it. 'Let it be hid': the play itself is seeled up.

6

SAFE

Macbeth

Enter LADY MACBETH, *and a* SERVANT

LADY MACBETH Is Banquo gone from court?
SERVANT Ay, madam, but returns again tonight.
LADY MACBETH Say to the king, I would attend his leisure
For a few words.
SERVANT   Madam, I will.   *Exit*
LADY MACBETH   Nought's had, all's spent
Where our desire is got without content.
'Tis safer to be that which we destroy
Than by destruction dwell in doubtful joy.

Enter MACBETH

How now, my lord, why do you keep alone,
Of sorriest fancies your companions making,
Using those thoughts which should indeed have died
With them they think on? Things without all remedy

	Should be without regard; what's done, is done.
MACBETH	We have scorched the snake, not killed it;
	She'll close, and be herself, whilst our poor malice
	Remains in danger of her former tooth.
	But let the frame of things disjoint, both the worlds suffer,
	Ere we will eat our meal in fear, and sleep
	In the affliction of these terrible dreams
	That shake us nightly. Better be with the dead
	Whom we, to gain our peace, have sent to peace,
	Than on the torture of the mind to lie
	In restless ecstasy. Duncan is in his grave.
	After life's fitful fever, he sleeps well;
	Treason has done his worst; nor steel nor poison,
	Malice domestic, foreign levy, nothing
	Can touch him further.
LADY MACBETH	Come on. Gentle my lord,
	Sleek o'er your rugged looks, be bright and jovial
	Among your guests tonight.
MACBETH	So shall I, love,
	And so I pray be you.

(3.2.1–30)

One of the most astonishing things about *Macbeth* is the way in which, through soliloquy, Shakespeare draws us into the minds of Macbeth and Lady Macbeth as individuals. Another is how, through dialogue, Shakespeare enables us to share the intimacy of their relationship as husband and wife. As I hope to make clear, the interrelation between Macbeth and Lady Macbeth borders on the magical or telepathic. In this sense it is subtly bound up with the more obviously magical or supernatural aspects of the play. This passage from around the middle of *Macbeth* is fascinating in all of these respects, but it is also crucial because it marks a decisive turn and disintegration in the couple's intimacy. Their conversation is centred on the crime they have committed, the murder of Duncan, the Scottish king, and the difficulties of living with the consequences – despite having now ostensibly got what they wanted, namely become king and queen. But it is also a passage in which we are acutely aware of what each character is concealing from the other. Each of them is now, in various ways, profoundly isolated.

Before looking at the passage in detail, let me establish a fuller sense of the context for what is going in Act 3 scene 2. *Macbeth* is generally reckoned to have been written in 1606, but there is no specific record of its having been performed before 1610 or 1611. There are oddities in the first published version of the text in the 1623 Folio. It contains material written by the playwright Thomas Middleton, in particular the witches' songs in Act 3 scene 5 ('Come away, come away') and Act 4 scene 1 ('Black spirits, etc.'). It is also generally reckoned that one of the scenes involving the witches and Hecate (Act 3 scene 5), along with Hecate's lines in Act 4 scene 1 (39–43), were not written by Shakespeare. *Macbeth* is by far the shortest of the 'great tragedies'. In the form in which it has come down to us (the First Folio being the only or nearest thing to an 'authoritative' text), it very possibly has bits missing as well as added.

As always in Shakespeare's plays, questions of the ghostly and magical are at work. This is true, to an unusual degree, of *Macbeth*. The play is steeped in the supernatural, the more than physical or, in Lady Macbeth's term, the 'metaphysical' (1.5.27). *Macbeth* starts with a scene of witchcraft and prophecy, amid thunder and lightning. Returning from battle,

Macbeth and his noble friend Banquo come across three witches on a heath who declare that Macbeth will become Thane of Cawdor and then King, whereas Banquo will 'get kings, though . . . be none' (1.3.65). Macbeth is duly rewarded for his battle performance with the title of 'Thane of Cawdor' by Duncan, the Scottish King. Duncan comes to stay at Macbeth's castle; that same night, with his wife as crucial, emboldening accomplice, he knifes Duncan to death. Duncan's sons, Malcolm and Donaldbain, flee the country. Macbeth becomes King but cannot forget the witches' predictions for Banquo: he hires a couple of killers to take out Banquo and his son Fleance. They murder the father, but Fleance escapes. Macbeth visits the witches who spirit up various apparitions that tell him three things: 'beware Macduff'; not to fear anyone 'of woman born' (4.1.70, 79); and not to fear defeat until 'Birnam Wood to high Dunsinane hill / Shall come against him' (4.1.92–3). When Macduff, the Thane of Fife, goes south to England to help mount an army against him, Macbeth has his wife and all his children murdered. In the meantime Lady Macbeth's mind has evidently become 'infected' and she takes her own life. As the Anglo-Scottish army led by Malcolm and Macduff approaches Dunsinane, Malcolm orders his men to cut down branches from the trees in Birnam Wood and use them as camouflage. The third of the prophecies declared by the apparitions summoned up by the witches is coming true. Macbeth fights on until he meets Macduff, who reveals that his mother died giving birth to him: literally, he was born of a corpse, not of a woman. Macduff decapitates him and the play concludes with Malcolm inviting all to Scone where he is to be crowned as the new Scottish King.

Act 3 scene 2 mostly comprises a conversation between

Macbeth and Lady Macbeth, taking place in some private area within their castle. In the immediately preceding scene Macbeth has had his cloak-and-dagger discussion with the two men who will, in the scene immediately after this, murder Banquo and botch the dispatch of his son. Banquo and Fleance have gone out for a ride, but Banquo is due back for dinner at the castle that evening. The apparently simple opening lines are subtly telling. The Queen's initial question ('Is Banquo gone from court?') establishes a sense of temporal continuity with the preceding scene: we carry on as if in (surreptitiously speeded-up) 'real time', switching from Macbeth at the end of Act 3 scene 1 concluding his discussion with Banquo's prospective murderers, to Lady Macbeth asking if Banquo has gone out riding yet. The figure of the servant divides as well as links husband and wife. There is a sense of formality, an emphasis on their not being together: 'Say to the king, I would attend his leisure / For a few words.'

While awaiting him, Lady Macbeth offers perhaps the most condensed soliloquy in the play. It comprises two related formulations. In the first she expresses the waste of energy ('all's spent') that results in having nothing ('Nought's had'), where we get what we want ('our desire') but it doesn't make us happy ('content'). Without naming him, she is clearly referring to the consequences of murdering Duncan. The second formulation likewise takes the impersonal form of a proverb, but again invites a more particular, murderous reading. Thus we read her as supposing that there is greater security (''Tis safer'), mentally as well as physically, in being the murdered one ('that which we destroy') than in being the murderers who as a result of their crime ('by destruction') live in a world in which all joy is questionable, suspect, full of apprehension.

'Safer' is ironic: it's better to be dead than in a state of doubt, or a murderee than a murderer. Some critics see the irony of 'safer' as extending also to a religious sense, as in 'saving one's soul'. 'Safe' and 'save' both derive from the Latin *salvus*, directly connecting also with the English word 'salvation'. Yet the word 'save', or cognate forms such as 'saved', 'saving', and so on, scarcely appears in the play. The only exception is the darkly ironic greeting, 'God save the king' (1.2.47), addressed to Duncan by the thane Ross, near the beginning of the play. This is not a play in which people get saved or save one another. Neither God nor any other agency can save the King. Macbeth cannot save his wife from going mad any more, apparently, than Macduff can save his wife and children from being butchered. One of the primary characteristics of Macbeth that has so disturbed spectators and readers over the past 400-odd years is the sense that he is fully aware of the damnable and terrible nature of what he does, but does it anyway. Duncan may go, in Macbeth's words, 'to heaven or to hell' (2.1.64): it doesn't ultimately seem to matter much to him one way or the other. The question of salvation appears to be irrelevant.

This almost complete elision of any religious 'saving' underscores the notion of safety, being safe, in the here and now. 'Safe', and related words such as 'safer', 'safely' and 'safety', all tend to emphasize the importance of this life now, the immediately physical. Throughout this short book I have been exploring how a single word in Shakespeare seems to conduct us into a reading of an entire play. 'Safe', in the case of *Macbeth*, irresistibly suggests itself here. This word conforms to the sort of wordplay that is characteristic of the play as a whole: wordplay in *Macbeth* has to do with the disturbing possibilities of 'equivocation' (5.5.42) and 'double sense' (5.8.20), such as Macbeth encounters in the deadly riddles of the witches and apparitions. Even on the first appearance of the word 'safe' in this play, Shakespeare seems to be playing with safety regulations: 'safe', in other words, seems troubled, ironic, unsafe. Having in an earlier aside entertained the thought of regicide – a 'thought' of 'murder', however fanciful or 'fantastical' (1.3.138) – Macbeth tells Duncan of his duty towards the King and his concern for 'doing everything / Safe toward your love and honour' (1.4.26–7), in other words doing the utmost to secure his safety and therefore be deserving of his love and honour. There is thus already a lurking suggestion here that to be 'safe' is to be dead. It is as if Macbeth (and the reader or audience) could already foresee the moment in Act 3 scene 4 when Macbeth, seeking confirmation that Banquo has been done for, asks 'But Banquo's safe?', and the First Murderer replies: 'Ay, my good lord: safe in a ditch he bides' (3.4.25–6). But even here, of course, 'safe' is not safe. Within moments of this exchange, Banquo reappears to Macbeth as a ghost. If Banquo is safe, it is as a ghost. There is a suggestion that 'safe' is a ghostly word, a word of ghost meaning. Correspondingly, Macbeth begins his major solil-oquy in Act 3 scene 1 with the words: 'To be thus is nothing, / But to be safely thus' (3.1.49–50), in other words to be king is nothing unless it is to be safely so. On stage or screen, the first 'thus' here might be played with some ges-ture towards his crown or other regal trimmings. Safety is apparently everything and yet what, in fact, is this elusive thing? As Hecate later declares: 'security / Is mortals' chiefest enemy' (3.5.32–3). The best way of being safe is never to suppose you are secure. There is no security in thinking you are safe.

At issue in these 'safe' cases (Macbeth's 'safe' and 'safely', Lady Macbeth's 'safer') is what critics have traditionally referred to as 'echoes', in other words the idea of one character or one moment in the text echoing another. In traditional critical terminology, Lady Macbeth's 'safer' here thus echoes Macbeth's earlier use of 'safe' and 'safely'. But the notion of echo in the context of *Macbeth* is in various ways misleading, equivocal, in a word *unsafe*. 'Echo' ordinarily suggests a chronological linear progression: first Macbeth uses a word, then Lady Macbeth echoes it. But Shakespeare's play disturbs this sense of order. This is indeed suggested by the only occasion in the play when the word 'echo' itself is used. Describing what he would do if his doctor could cure his country, could 'purge it to a sound and pristine health', Macbeth tells him: 'I would applaud thee to the very echo / That should applaud again' (5.3.54–5). 'Echo' here ceases to comprise identifiable source and repetition or response: instead we are given a sort of mad applause, applauding 'the very echo'. It is no longer possible to say with certainty where or when this echo begins (again). The logic of echo in the context of *Macbeth* is not simply or necessarily linear: the 'first' appearance of a word, phrase or image can respond to, or be haunted by, its apparently 'later' appearance. Madness and death, haunting and destruction resonate in the word 'safe' from the beginning. This strange effect of the after before, of what comes later coming earlier, is fundamental to the play as a whole. It is intimately linked up with how the witches' prophecies come true – how they structure the narrative – and with the sense of experiencing (in feeling, fantasy or reading) the future in the present, or what Lady Macbeth calls '[t]he future in the instant' (1.5.56).

There is another strange thing about echoes in *Macbeth*. They lead us, or rather they transpire to have led us in the dark from the start, into a space of magical thinking or telepathy. This is especially significant for an appreciation of the peculiarly intense relationship between Macbeth and Lady Macbeth; but the question of echoes is also, from the beginning, bound up with the question of witchcraft, magic and the supernatural. In the opening lines of the play the three witches together chant: 'Fair is foul, and foul is fair' (1.1.12). A short while after this, Macbeth and Banquo come by and we hear Macbeth's first words on stage: 'So foul and fair a day I have not seen' (1.3.36). It is as if his speech is not his own, as if some logic of magical thinking or telepathy is already in effect. Later in the play, indeed, when he returns to consult the witches and is shown the first apparition (the helmeted head of a man) and starts to address it ('Tell me, thou unknown power . . .'), the First Witch bluntly interrupts him: 'He knows thy thought; / Hear his speech, but say thou nought' (4.1.68–9). All of this might seem to run counter to Duncan's celebrated (if deeply ironic) remark, made just prior to the entrance of Macbeth: 'There's no art / To find the mind's construction in the face' (1.4.11–12). But as I have been suggesting at various points in this book, magical or telepathic knowledge is everywhere in Shakespeare. It is inherent in his playwriting, most obviously in the form of the numerous asides or soliloquies. We repeatedly get to be in the position of the apparition, to know a character's innermost thoughts. But such magical knowledge is also hinted at in subtler and more intricate ways, in the shifts and drifts of words, phrases and images between characters, apparently without the characters' own awareness.

Above all there are the peculiar kinds of rapport (often

unspoken) between Macbeth and Lady Macbeth. Her brief soliloquy early in Act 3 scene 2 enables us to know not only what she is thinking and feeling, but also that she is not being entirely honest in what she says when her husband enters the room: 'How now, my lord, why do you keep alone, / Of sorriest fancies your companions making . . .?' We know, in other words, that it is *she* who has been entertaining the most sad and wretched imaginings ('sorriest fancies'). It is she who has just been making imaginary associations with 'that which we destroy'. 'Fancies' carries strong connotations of delusion or hallucination and in this context closely resembles what Brutus, in *Julius Caesar*, calls a phantasma. The word occurs only twice in the play: it returns for one final appearance near the end, when the Scottish doctor describes Lady Macbeth as being 'troubled with thick-coming fancies' (5.3.39). The word 'fancies' is, eerily, hers and not hers. And, of course, it is attributed to Macbeth as well.

When Macbeth enters, she knows it is not a matter of 'attend[ing] his leisure'. ('Leisure' here becomes one of the most ironic words in the play.) She doesn't have to ask. She evidently knows what he is thinking. Her attempt to comfort her husband in Act 3 scene 2 is charged with pathos. The passage as a whole elicits complicated feelings and impressions in us. Shakespeare's ability to arouse sympathy, as well as antipathy, for a couple of fiendish criminals is indissociably linked to the strange interior knowledge, the quasi-telepathic intimacy we experience. Lady Macbeth appears to know that he is 'Using [entertaining, making himself accustomed to] those thoughts which should indeed have died / With them they think on'. Poignantly recognizing or reading in him the very thoughts she herself has just been privately articulating, Lady Macbeth at the same time recalls a strangely shared conception of thoughts as murderous, deadly or mortal. In Act 1 Macbeth speaks, in an aside, of entertaining 'horrible imaginings' of regicide, referring to '[his] thought, whose murder yet is but fantastical' (1.3.137–8); and in her own soliloquy shortly after this, Lady Macbeth invokes 'you spirits / That tend on mortal [i.e. murderous, deadly] thoughts' (1.5.38–9). Neither witnessed the other's speech, but both independently think thought as murder or as murderous. But thoughts are not people: even as she speaks of making one's companions thoughts that should have died, thoughts that ought to be dead and buried, Lady Macbeth generates fancies. It is as if her words themselves become gravely trapped in the very process of trying to dismiss what is beyond 'all remedy'.

The final formulation 'what's done, is done' is, apparently, final – tautologically simple. But it is also fantastically complex, a double appearance of what is perhaps the most enigmatically repeated, curiously echoey word in the play. *Macbeth* seems never to be done with 'done'. The word is sounded in the name Duncan, and can perhaps be heard to resonate also in Macbeth's evocation of a darkness in which 'the eye fears when it is done to see' (1.4.53) or Lady Macbeth's summoning up 'the dunnest [i.e. murkiest] smoke of hell' (1.5.49). In the context of this play it is impossible to be sure *when* anything (and above all a murder) is done. The time of the doing is always at odds with itself, and *what* is done is apparently never completely or purely done. The murder (or assassination) is not just something that happens and is then all over and done with. However much Lady Macbeth might want to claim that 'what's done, is done', she and her husband are in fact wracked and haunted by their murderous deed till their deaths. The doing of the deed in a sense never ends. In a nightmarish or phantasma-like way, the crime is at once something that cannot be 'undone' and yet also (in its haunting enormity and after-effects) something that carries on happening.

The word 'done' occurs some thirty-five times in the play. It repeats, reverberates, resounds like a knell, summoning strange kinds of communication between one speech or scene or character and another. In particular, Lady Macbeth's 'what's done, is done' suggests an eerie connection with the opening of Macbeth's soliloquy in Act 1 scene 7, in which he contemplates Duncan's murder: 'If it were done when 'tis done, then 'twere well / It were done quickly . . .' (1.7.1–2). But a murder is never timely. For the murderer or his accomplice, in particular, it seems to have (in Macbeth's ironically astute words prior to the deed) no 'be-all [and] end-all' (1.7.5). It haunts thinking, it is always there. It keeps coming back, in ghostly and traumatic fashion, to be thought again. In the extraordinary sleepwalking scene in Act 5, Lady Macbeth beckons her imagined husband to bed with the words: 'Come, come, come, come, give me your hand; what's done cannot be undone' (5.1.57–8). Her very reciting of the earlier phrase ('what's done, is done') undoes the certainty of this 'done'. Lady Macbeth's somniloquent reiterations in her final stage appearance indeed horrifyingly underscore the sense that the doing of the deed is still going on, that she will never be done with washing her hands of it, and that we, by implication, will perhaps never be done with reading or thinking about it.

'We have scorched the snake, not killed it': Macbeth's interjection passionately denounces any supposition that 'what's done, is done'. 'Scorched' here has the (now obsolete) sense of 'slashed', 'scored', 'gashed'. The image is of having failed to slash or gash it thoroughly enough. Macbeth talks of killing (or not yet having managed to kill), though the snake here is a disturbingly slippery figure. The snake refers not simply to Duncan, but Banquo and Banquo's son Fleance, as well as Duncan's sons, Malcolm and Donaldbain, and indeed perhaps more generally Duncan's friends and allies. 'It', moreover, quickly slides into 'she': 'She'll close, and be herself', in other words the gash will close up and the snake return to her former state. The gendering of the snake as female is intriguing; it prevents any straightforward identification of the snake with a specific male (such as Duncan), while also hinting at a figure of proliferating or birth-giving powers. Later that evening, when he hears from the First Murderer that Banquo is 'safe in a ditch' but Fleance got away, Macbeth remarks: 'There the grown serpent lies; the worm that's fled / Hath nature that in time will venom breed, / No teeth for th' present' (3.4.26–31). His word here for Fleance, 'worm', is generally understood to mean 'small serpent', but there is also a suggestion of 'grub': a power of generating and regenerating would appear to be inscribed in Macbeth's 'snake' from the start.

Appositely but strangely, the earliest serpentine reference in the play is to Macbeth himself. In murderous anticipation of Duncan's arrival at their castle, Lady Macbeth tells her husband: 'bear welcome in your eye, / Your hand, your tongue; look like th'innocent flower, / But be the serpent under't' (1.5.62–4). At the end of the passage we are considering in Act 3 scene 2, there is a gentler, more poignant version of the flower and serpent, when she encourages Macbeth to look otherwise than how he feels: 'Sleek o'er your rugged looks, be bright and jovial / Among your guests tonight.' And Macbeth replies by exhorting her likewise ('So

shall I, love, / And so I pray be you'). Everything now seems
to be a matter of cover-up and acting, even between husband
and wife. Besides knowing Lady Macbeth's thoughts (which
she is attempting to conceal from her husband), we also
know that Macbeth is concealing things from her. In particular, he is not telling her that he has already given
instructions for the murder of Banquo and Fleance. There is
an intimacy here, in other words, that is strangely ours as
readers or spectators, as much as or even more than it is an
intimacy between the characters. There is something imposing, even painful, about Macbeth's now acting alone, but in
other respects his speech in this passage scarcely encourages
our sympathy. If we do not take further violent action, he
suggests, 'our poor malice / Remains in danger of her
former tooth' (i.e. in danger of the snake's continuing capacity for biting and poisoning). The 'our' is provoking: it is not
clear whether he means himself and Lady Macbeth or simply
himself (i.e. a royal 'our'). 'Poor malice' (insufficient wicked-
ness) is a kind of oxymoron verging on grim humour. It is as
if he expects sympathy on account of having been deprived
of not yet doing enough harm.

   Macbeth makes a startlingly abrupt turn, twist or disjoining
in his speech. The snake disappears into the universal image of
'the frame of things': 'But let the frame of things disjoint, both
the worlds suffer, / Ere we will eat our meal in fear, and sleep
/ In the affliction of these terrible dreams / That shake us nightly.'
Let the universe fall apart, let both the terrestrial and celestial
worlds be destroyed, so long as it means we don't have to eat in
a state of fright and be afflicted by these nightmares. This is, in
an unnervingly literal, apocalyptic form, 'Anything for a good
night's sleep'. The little preposition concerned with time ('ere',
i.e. 'before') is crucial to the strangeness of these lines. It seems

as if this 'ere', bolstered by the future tense 'will', refers to
meals and nightmares that have not yet happened; but the deictic 'these' and the constancy of the 'nightly' (every night)
suggest that they have already been happening for some time.
'Ere' trammels up past, present and future. The references to
'our meal' and 'terrible dreams' are also creepily predictive of
the haunted dinner later the same day and of Lady Macbeth's
mind-dissolving, sleepwalking nightmares.

The earlier sense of the royal 'we' seems now to be more
clearly a terrifying yet intimate marital 'we' ('our meal', 'dreams
/ That shake us'). We are drawn back here to the sense of
Macbeth and Lady Macbeth as two creatures disjointed in
one or, in Sigmund Freud's striking phrase, as 'two disunited
parts of a single psychical individuality'.[7] They seem to share
and be shaken by the same dreams: the 'these' ('*these* terrible
dreams') implies she knows exactly what he is talking about.
This sense of a peculiarly intense psychical rapport is then
accentuated: 'Better be with the dead / Whom we, to gain
our peace, have sent to peace . . .' It is as if he were reading
her mind: ''Tis safer to be that which we destroy.' Like 'safe',
'peace' figures as an antithetical word, an unsafe single word
of double sense, signifying both 'satisfaction' (or 'ambition')
and 'death'.

Macbeth is perhaps Shakespeare's least sexual play. This is as
close as we come to a bedroom scene. Husband and wife
apparently lie 'on the torture of the mind . . . / In restless
ecstasy', in other words on a bed like a torture rack, restlessly
beside themselves. (There is apparent play here on the word
'ecstasy' as, literally, a state outside or beside oneself, in a
frenzy of fear or some other form of mental alienation.)
Life, in Macbeth's phrase, is a 'fitful fever'. This is, according
to the *OED*, the first recorded use of the word 'fitful' in the

history of the English language. Macbeth applies the phrase 'fitful fever' to Duncan, though it is far more obviously appropriate to himself and his wife. Recurrent attacks or fits are precisely what he himself experiences later this same day, when he hears that Fleance has escaped ('Then comes my fit again', he exclaims: 3.4.21) and when he sees the Ghost of Banquo (in a 'fit' that is 'momentary', according to Lady Macbeth, but which then recurs, as if it were 'a thing of custom', after the Ghost has exited and reappeared: see 3.4.55, 97).

It is all right for Duncan, he is a good sleeper. Macbeth here adds another restless turn to one of the most disturbed words in the play, 'sleep'. It is not simply a matter of saying that death is a sleep; the phrase 'he sleeps well' suggests something better than merely being dead. There is nothing else that can be *done* to Duncan. He is invulnerable to everything, whether treason, swords or daggers, poison, the envy or hatred of his fellow Scots, or armies levied outside Scotland. The final words of Macbeth's speech ('nothing / Can touch him further') para-doxically recall and in some respects counter the image of the scorched snake with which he began. Shakespeare's play is full of scorching – from the inflicting of Duncan's 'gashed stabs [that] looked like a breach in nature' (2.3.106) to the 'twenty trenchèd gashes on [Banquo's] head' (3.4.27) to the more general 'gash / . . . added to [Scotland's] wounds' with 'each new day' (4.3.40–41). Above all, it is a terrifying account of the impossibility of ever being vicious and malicious enough, of ever doing enough damage and harm to ensure one's complete 'safety'. There is a kind of madness in this logic of doing wrong, of more violence making things safer. Macbeth and Lady Macbeth remain, in his phrase, 'unsafe the while' (3.2.32). At the very end of Act 3 scene 2, he seeks to provide a rationale for his next 'deed of dreadful note' (3.2.44): 'Things bad begun, make strong themselves by ill' (3.2.55). Critics often compare this to a Latin aphorism in Seneca's *Agamemnon* ('per scelera semper sceleribus tutum est iter': 'the safe way for crime is through crime') and to an English proverb, 'Crimes are made secure by greater crime'. It is deeply disturbing. Crime leads to more crime, abuse begets abuse, and so on. *Macbeth* might also prompt us to think about the limits, and even the madness, of the pursuit of being 'safe' in a less obviously criminal context (moving towards a police state, for instance, in the name of 'national security' or a 'war on terror').

What, finally, is 'safe'? For all its apparently entrenched concern with slashing, gashing, scorching and hacking – 'I'll fight till from my bones my flesh be hacked' (5.3.32) is how Macbeth gruesomely pictures his determination, shortly before his final battle – Shakespeare's play is perhaps just as much about what cannot be touched or wounded. There is in *Macbeth*, and correspondingly also in *Antony and Cleopatra* and *The Tempest* (as we will see in the next chapter), a significant affirmation of air, of air itself as strangely *safe*. Very near the end of the play, mocking Macduff's 'keen sword', Macbeth speaks of bearing 'a charmèd life which must not yield / To one of woman born'. Ironically and erroneously, he compares himself in his invulnerabilty to what he calls 'the intrenchant air' (5.8.9–13). 'Intrenchant', a word that occurs nowhere else in Shakespeare's writings, can be glossed as 'uncuttable', 'beyond gashing', 'invulnerable'. It recalls the 'air-drawn dagger' (3.4.62), the hallucinated 'dagger of the mind' (2.1.38) that leads Macbeth on the path to his destruction, as well as the airy vision of the invulnerable, untouchable Ghost of Banquo himself. 'Air' is strange. It is of course 'ere' –

the homophone that sounds the foretelling, prophetic dimensions of the play. And it is a word recurrently associated with the witches. As Macbeth tells Lady Macbeth in a letter: 'When I burned in desire to question them further, they made themselves air, into which they vanished' (1.5.3–5). It is air into which the witches will have 'vanished' (1.3.78–9) – along with the very play of which they are a part.

7

NOD

Antony and Cleopatra

Need death be something to fear? Might dying not be affirmative, beautiful, erotic? Might it not dissolve the very idea of seriousness? Shakespeare's *Antony and Cleopatra* is generally thought to have been written in 1606 and was first published in the 1623 Folio under the title 'The Tragedie of Anthonie, and Cleopatra'. Yet it is not a tragedy in the way that we might think of *Hamlet*, *Othello*, *King Lear* or *Macbeth* as tragedies. *Antony and Cleopatra* seems to work through its tragic structure and come out somewhere on the other side, in a space of strange exhilaration, playfulness and joy. It is not by chance that, more than in any other of his works, Shakespeare plays with the connotations of 'death' and 'dying' as sexual climax and coming. And it seems, in *Antony and Cleopatra*, that there is always a chance of coming again, an ecstatic anticipation of love beyond death. By comparison, the earlier tragedy *Romeo and Juliet* (1595) – for all the erotic intensity in the depiction of its eponymous lovers – comes to a halt at death. Romeo drinks poison then kisses Juliet (whom he erroneously believes to be dead already) for the final time: 'The drugs are quick! Thus with a kiss I die' (5.3.120). Very soon after this, Juliet takes Romeo's dagger and contentedly plunges it into herself: 'O happy dagger, / This [i.e. my body] is thy sheath! There rust, and let me die' (5.3.168–9). Romeo Montague and Juliet Capulet, caput. When writing *Antony and Cleopatra*, Shakespeare was an older man, his hero and heroine an older couple. Antony speaks of his hair as a 'mingl[ing]' of 'grey' with 'younger brown' (4.8.19–20); Cleopatra is no longer in her 'salad days, / When [she] was green [immature] in judgement' (1.5.76–7). This perhaps makes the eroticism and affirmation surrounding their death all the more extraordinary. Preparing to fall on his sword, Antony declares, 'I will be / A bridegroom in my death and run into't / As to a lover's bed' (4.14.99–101). Cleopatra out-does him and every other character in English literature, however, in her erotic affirmations on her death. She cannot wait to 'come' to her lover in the afterworld, to 'meet the curlèd [curly-locked] Antony' and have the 'heaven' of his 'kiss' (5.2.295–7). She cannot apply a poisonous asp to her breast fast enough. 'Come,' she tells it, 'Poor venomous fool, / Be angry, and dispatch.' Dying becomes one further orgasmic experience prior to being reunited with Antony. Any sense of death as something unjust, terrible or terrifying (the more usual emphasis in Shakespeare's tragedies) has dissolved.

Like *Julius Caesar*, Shakespeare's *Antony and Cleopatra* is deeply indebted to Sir Thomas North's translation of Plutarch's *Lives of the Noble Grecians and Romans* (1579). He draws the bulk of the historical narrative and appropriates many details in verbatim or near verbatim fashion, especially from the Life of Marcus Antonius. Although our general image of *Antony and Cleopatra* today is deeply dependent on

Shakespeare's play, it is nevertheless worth stressing that in the early seventeenth century his play was also in competition with various other versions of an already famous story. These included the Countess of Pembroke's *The Tragedy of Antony* (1590, published in 1592 and 1595), which was her translation of Robert Garnier's *Antoine* (1578), and Samuel Daniel's *The Tragedy of Cleopatra* (written in 1594, published in revised versions in 1599 and 1607). Shakespeare modifies Plutarch's account in numerous ways, condensing the time frame and producing a picture of events that is a great deal more sympathetic to Cleopatra than Plutarch's. Shakespeare at once upholds, unsettles and transforms the classical emphasis on Rome as the embodiment of orderliness, moral virtue and reason, and Egypt as passion, excess and unreason.

The play is set in the period following Julius Caesar's assassination (44 BC), when the world is ruled by three men, the triumvirs Mark Antony, Lepidus and Octavius Caesar (Caesar's great nephew). Antony is in command of the East, which is how he comes to see and fall in love with Cleopatra, Queen of Egypt. In a scintillating scattering of scenes, some long, some very short, the action shifts between Alexandria and Rome, the vicinity of Naples (Misenum) and an unspecific location in the Middle East, Athens and Actium in Greece, where the fate of the world is being determined by a few characters and the battles in which they are involved. The final stages of the tragedy (from Act 3 scene 11 onwards) are set in and around Alexandria. The action culminates in the Battle of Actium (31 BC) and the Battle of Alexandria (30 BC), waged by the armies of Octavius Caesar against those of Antony and Cleopatra. For all the historical significance of these events, however, Shakespeare maintains spectacular focus on Antony and Cleopatra themselves. It is through their passion – their anger as well as their sexual desire – that we experience what happens. In military and political terms, Caesar wins; but at the same time, more strikingly, he is a figure to be mocked – in Cleopatra's pronouncement, an 'ass / Unpolicied [outwitted or outmanoeuvred]' (5.2.301–2).

Let us pick things up close to the end, namely at the opening of Act 4 scene 14. Here, in just a dozen or so lines, we encounter one of the most extraordinary descriptions of the human body, identity, self and dissolution, anywhere in Shakespeare's writings. A little earlier, Enobarbus, Antony's most intimate and dedicated follower ('one ever near [Antony]', as an unnamed soldier describes him: 4.5.7), has deserted him and gone over to Caesar's camp. We now know (though Antony does not) that Enobarbus has died, apparently of grief: his mortified last words are 'O Antony! O Antony!' (4.10.23). More generally, the Battle of Alexandria has been lost and Antony is convinced that Cleopatra has betrayed him. He believes that she has treacherously sided with Caesar and has, as he puts it, '[b]eguiled [charmed and cheated] me to the very heart of loss' (4.12.29). Antony attributes the power of witchcraft or the supernatural to this disastrous turn in events. He repeatedly refers to Cleopatra as a witch or 'charm' (4.12.16, 25), an enchantment or 'spell' (4.12.30). It is the end, in his eyes: 'O sun, thy uprise shall I see no more' (4.12.18). Cleopatra then enters. For her part, she cannot understand: 'Why is my lord enraged against his love?' (4.12.31). But Antony seems only to be able to envisage her paying with her life for what she has apparently done: 'The witch shall die' (4.12.47). She is so frightened by his 'mad' behaviour that she locks herself in the 'monument' – or 'tomb', as North's *Plutarch* also calls it – where she herself will soon enough die. She then orders Mardian, her eunuch, to 'go tell [Antony] I have slain myself / . . . / And bring me how he takes my death' (4.13.1–10). It is at this point that we shift back to Antony, alone but for his still-loyal follower Eros:

Enter ANTONY *and* EROS

ANTONY	Eros, thou yet behold'st me?
EROS	Ay, noble lord.
ANTONY	Sometime we see a cloud that's dragonish,
	A vapour sometime like a bear or lion,
	A towered citadel, a pendent rock,
	A forkèd mountain, or blue promontory
	With trees upon't that nod unto the world
	And mock our eyes with air. Thou hast seen these signs;
	They are black vesper's pageants.
EROS	Ay, my lord.
ANTONY	That which is now a horse, even with a thought
	The rack dislimns and makes it indistinct
	As water is in water.
EROS	It does, my lord.
ANTONY	My good knave Eros, now thy captain is
	Even such a body. Here I am Antony,
	Yet cannot hold this visible shape, my knave.

(4.14.1–14)

Can you still see me, Eros? We must suppose that Antony is perfectly visible at this point and that Eros answers 'Ay, noble lord', without understanding why his master should ask such a thing. Antony renders his strange question intelligible only at the end of these dozen or so lines, during which he evokes the most manifestly baseless sequence of imaginary figures in what is perhaps Shakespeare's most exuberantly imaginative play. The setting is a room in Cleopatra's palace at Alexandria. In the following few lines (from 'Sometime we see a cloud' to 'mock our eyes with air'), Antony might gesture upwards towards the clouds. Whether or not the passage is staged (or imagined) within sight of a cloudy open sky, these ever-changing shapes (like a dragon, a bear, a lion, and so on) figure the shifting, fleeting, changing scenes of the play itself. In part we share Eros's sense of bafflement at his master's speech. Has he indeed gone mad? But Antony's flight of thought here also offers the most sustained meditation on what lies at the heart of Shakespeare's play, namely transformation, becoming, dissolving, melting, discandying, vanishing, dying, losing oneself.

'Sometime,' Antony says, suggesting a single occasion, 'we see a cloud that's dragonish.' Almost imperceptibly, through this phrase 'we see', the speaker has drifted into the same place as Eros, as the one who beholds. Antony says 'a cloud' but then 'a vapour': are these the same thing? In some ways the passage seems to be about a dissolving of the identities and links between words themselves. Syntax cannot hold. Words fall apart. 'Vapour' and 'cloud' interchange but are irreducibly different. One seems to dissolve into the other. At the same time there is a logic to their ordering. Quite apart from any obvious messing up of metre, it would be odd for Antony to say 'vapour' first and 'cloud' second. 'Cloud' is the more familiar term, even in Shakespearean English. 'Cloud' also has connotations of something bulkier, more visible. It is as if language itself drifts and cascades, from cloud to vapour.

In the air here are the eerie effects of specific words or images that pass, in significant and ramifying fashion, from one character to another, one scene to another, without any character's apparent knowledge. Near the end of the play, after Antony has died, as if she had heard him talking about 'cloud' and 'vapour', Cleopatra contemplates what will happen if she does not commit suicide. She evokes for her attendant Iras the disgusting humiliation of being led in triumph into Rome in the presence of all the plebeians. They will, she says, 'uplift us to the view. In their thick breaths, / Rank of gross diet, shall we be enclouded / And forced to drink their vapour' (5.2.210–12). The common Roman people depend on a 'gross diet' that makes them smell bad ('rank'). In *Julius Caesar*, likewise, the plebeians are held to have 'stinking breath' (1.2.241). Cleopatra's is the first and only use of the verb 'to encloud' in Shakespeare. She splutters out the variations ('thick breath', 'enclouded', 'vapour') for an enclouded, encrowded image of having to inhale (or 'drink') the people's foul breath. 'Vapour' for Cleopatra, then, is 'breath'. Besides its appearance in Antony's 'cloud' lines, this is the only other instance of the word 'vapour' in the play. Cleopatra's images of 'cloud' and 'vapour' suggest the most base and claustrophobic fate, the inverse of Antony's airy, drifting and expansive vision. The two accounts at once cross and pass into one another.

'Sometime we see a cloud that's dragonish': Antony's first example of what a cloud might look like is also the most monstrous and fantastical. This is also the only cloud described by way of the verbal tail or suffix, '-ish' (signifying 'somewhat', 'like', 'resembling'). The word 'dragonish' appears just once in Shakespeare's writings and, in the sense of 'Somewhat like a dragon in shape', at least according to the *OED*, has no recorded usage in English before *Antony and Cleopatra*. What are we looking at when we see a 'dragonish' cloud? There is perhaps a play here on the association between the figure of the dragon and the idea of watchfulness. The *OED* points out that the etymology of 'dragon' is often referred back to the Ancient Greek *edrakon*, a form of the verb *derkesthai*, 'to see clearly'. The clouds are watching you. Seeing has shifted again. The strange suggestiveness of 'dragonish' also recalls the monstrous image conjured by Antony in his enraged outburst at Cleopatra just a few moments earlier. Here he had threatened to 'blemish Caesar's triumph' by doing the job for him. Antony's image of Cleopatra being 'hoist[ed] . . . up' by Caesar and shown 'most monster-like' (most freak-like or monstrous) (4.12.34–5) to the plebeians in Rome seems to show up in mutant form in the dragonish cloud, before finally gathering in Cleopatra's image of being 'uplift[ed] to the view' and 'enclouded' in 'vapour'.

'Sometime we see a cloud . . . / A vapour sometime like a bear or lion, / A towered citadel, a pendent rock, / A forkèd mountain . . .' The second 'sometime' is like but not the same as the first: governing the potentially interminable outpouring of what a cloud might look like, it is, at once more explicitly and more uncertainly, singular and plural. Syntax becomes a 'sometime' thing. The '-ish' vanishes into a 'like' ('like a bear or lion'), and the 'like' likewise seems to give way, becoming lost in the piling up of imagined cloud formations that follow. Antony evokes a series of images that become increasingly distant and detached from that 'like': a castle or fortress with towers, an overhanging rock, a mountain with two or more peaks . . . The sense of simile, comparison and resemblance ('like') has virtually dissolved by the time we reach the 'blue promontory', perhaps the most complex and transfixing image in Antony's cloudscape. This headland seems to stick out, at the end, as if projecting another world. There is something paradoxical about the 'blue', a word perhaps more likely to be associated with the sky itself than with what is in the sky. And the trees are strange, flickeringly anthropomorphic, vaporous, skyey trees that, not of this world, 'nod unto the world'.

To nod is to make a downward motion of the head, understood as a gesture of assent or affirmation, greeting or command. To nod can also be to let the head drop in weariness or dozing, or to lean over as if about to fall asleep. A nod can be the movement of the head or a slight bow in accordance with such gestures. 'Nod' is a little word, a small movement, an apparently humble thing. Yet it accommodates a surprising range of connotations. It can be imperious or deferential, detached or intimate, confiding or cryptic, menacing or seductive, vigilant or sleepy. And it will perhaps come as little surprise to find that Shakespeare plays on all these possibilities. Indeed, in accordance with the remarkable way in which his language operates, 'nod' seems to become a nodal point, nodding towards a reading of the entire textual network in which it appears. 'Nod' turns up in all sorts of places in Shakespeare. It figures in the first scene of what is conventionally thought of as his first play, *The Two Gentlemen of Verona* (1590–91), where it is playfully connected up with the 'ay' (and 'I' and 'eye') to make a verbal fool, a 'nod-ay' or 'noddy':

PROTEUS   But what said she?
SPEED   [*nods, then says*] Ay.
PROTEUS   Nod-ay? Why, that's 'noddy'.
SPEED   You mistook, sir. I say she did nod, and you ask me if she did nod, and I say 'Ay'.
PROTEUS   And that set together is 'noddy'.

(1.1.104–9)

In *Julius Caesar*, in the passage quoted earlier in this book, 'nod' is linked with sleep. The young musician Lucio is liable to 'nod' and break his instrument (4.3.271). In *Macbeth* the nod is identified with substitution, spectrality, and a menacing silence. Terrified by the Ghost of Banquo sitting in his own place at the dinner table, Macbeth exclaims: 'If thou canst nod, speak too' (3.4.70).

In Act 4 scene 14 of *Antony and Cleopatra*, 'nod' primarily refers to the bending downwards or forwards of imaginary trees. This somewhat hypnotic, sleepy image of plants recalls Oberon's enchanting description, in *A Midsummer Night's Dream*, of where Titania sleeps: 'I know a bank where the wild thyme blows, / Where oxlips and the nodding violet grows . . .' (2.1.249–50). But the trees in *Antony and Cleopatra* are stranger. Their nodding seems at once more eerie and more human, especially with the subsequent verb 'mock' ('trees . . . that nod unto the world / And mock . . .'). Moreover, the verb 'to nod' has made an intriguing couple of appearances earlier in the play. Caesar uses the word contemptuously when telling his sister Octavia (whom Antony had married for political reasons) that Antony is not in Athens, where she supposes him to be: 'No, my most wrongèd sister, Cleopatra / Hath nodded him to her. He hath given his empire / Up to a whore . . .' (3.6.67–9). In this context 'nod' signifies summoning by a nod. Caesar evokes a kind of lascivious physicality; the 'whore' does not even have to speak, merely nod Antony to her. And there is also perhaps, bound into Caesar's 'nodded', a hint of enchantment, of Antony in thrall, blindly obeying, giving up his empire to her. Of course Antony has not heard Caesar use the word in this fashion, and yet (for the reader or listener) his use of it seems strangely inflected by Caesar's. It is a false nodding, that 'mock[s] our eyes with air'. The nodding trees trick and deceive, like the 'whore' (4.12.13) Antony himself now sees Cleopatra as being. There is another 'nod', however, even earlier in the play. During a period when Antony and Cleopatra are separated from one another, Alexas in the role of messenger brings her a pearl that Antony has given her, together with his reported message: 'I will piece / Her opulent throne with kingdoms. All the East, / Say thou, shall call her mistress.' Then Alexas adds: 'So he nodded, / And soberly did mount an arm-gaunt steed [a lean and hardened battle-horse]' (1.5.47–50). Caesar's image of Cleopatra's nodding is already traced by Antony's nodding. If Cleopatra nods to Antony, he also nods to her. Something of their extraordinary passion and rapport with one another is communicated, speechlessly, cryptically, through the shifting play of this little word.

In Antony's strange and drifting speech, the trees nod and 'mock our eyes with air'. What nods? What mocks? Are the 'trees' there or are they 'air'? 'Nod' seems to make a mockery of sense. 'Mock' here anticipates the auditory fancy or phantasma Cleopatra reports as she approaches death: 'Methinks I hear / Antony call ... / I hear him mock / The luck of Caesar' (5.2.277–80). But it also recalls the stress on Antony's mocking in North's *Plutarch*: Antony, we are told, 'was as well contented to be mocked as to mock others'. And it calls to mind Hamlet's mockery of Polonius:

HAMLET   Do you see yonder cloud that's almost in shape of a camel?
POLONIUS By th' mass, and it's like a camel indeed.
HAMLET   Methinks it is like a weasel.
POLONIUS It is backed like a weasel.
HAMLET   Or like a whale?
POLONIUS Very like a whale.

(*Hamlet*, 3.2.358–64)

It is a brutally funny exchange. It could go on for ever. There are many examples of clouds being described in terms of different animals and natural objects, in literary and other works, from Shakespeare to as far back as the play entitled *Nubes* (or 'The Clouds') by Aristophanes (*c*.448–*c*.388 BC). What makes the account in *Antony and Cleopatra* distinctive and apparently original is that these clouds are figuring the dissolution of the very identity of the speaker, Antony himself.

You have seen these images or portents, Antony tells Eros. The clouds that he has been conjuring up are no longer simply clouds, but 'signs'. They are *to be read*. There is an uncertain mingling of mockery and portentousness. 'They are black vesper's pageants': these five words shadow forth the protean magnificence and elusive compression of Shakespeare's play. Eros then says, 'Ay, my lord', but again it is not clear what he is assenting to. There is a rather distracted, dreamy, noddy quality to the contribution of Eros in this passage. Antony appears to be saying that these clouds are the spectacular displays, the dramatic scenes of dark evening, the sort of thing one sometimes sees when the sun is going down. We might wonder at the retrospective effects of this comment, as it prompts us to visualize all the preceding cloud images, up to the 'blue promontory', in a new and more nocturnal hue. Time, then, has shifted on. Evening has apparently already descended. The implied movement from light (seeing intricately detailed shapes of clouds, colour, nodding) to night ('black vesper') is a sombre reversal of the sort of Egyptian revelry recalled by Enobarbus when he says: 'we did sleep day out of countenance, and made the night light with drinking' (2.2.189–90). 'Black vesper' is, in any case, a peculiar juxtaposition: if 'vesper' (from the Latin *vesper*, 'evening', related to the ancient Greek *Hesperos*) were truly 'black', we might reasonably suppose it would no longer be itself, but night. Elsewhere in the play, for example, Lepidus speaks of 'night's blackness' (1.4.13). Most darkly, Antony's use of the word 'black' brings in death. A link is thus made with his declaration, in the line we encountered earlier: 'O sun, thy uprise shall I see no more' (4.12.18). There is also a prefiguring here of Iras's deathly comment, in the final scene of the play: 'The bright day is done, / And we are for the dark' (5.2.192–3).

Above all, there is the question of Antony's tone when he says, apropos 'these signs', 'They are black vesper's pageants.' Is he being ironic or fanciful or superstitiously anxious or darkly resigned or indeed despairing? The impression of a nodding mockery of sense remains. As always, the question of how to read Shakespeare is startlingly open. Antony's regal yet cryptic formulation doubtless has connotations of funerals and perhaps the Triumph of Death. With 'black' there is also, I think, a hint of the witchcraft noted earlier, recalling the sense of this adjective, for example, in the phrase 'night's black agents' in *Macbeth* (3.2.53). The primary sense of 'pageants', however, is theatrical. 'Pageants' originally referred to the movable stages on which medieval Miracle Plays were performed, but already, by Shakespeare's time, the word had come to mean the plays themselves or, more generally, theatrical spectacles and entertainments. Antony's is thus a meditation not only on clouds or on himself but also on the vesperal character of theatre itself. There is a striking correspondence between this passage of *Antony and Cleopatra* and Prospero's words in *The Tempest* (1611) following the presentation of a magical pageant (a kind of play-within-the-play). Prospero speaks of all the actors having 'melted into air', and of how everything, including 'the great globe itself', 'shall dissolve; / And, like this insubstantial pageant faded, / Leave not a rack behind' (4.1.150–56). The 'globe' here is at once the world and the theatre of that name, the Globe in which Shakespeare and his fellow actors performed, and which in its reconstructed form on London's South Bank can still be visited today. 'This insubstantial pageant' is the theatrical-spectacle-within-the-play, but it is also Shakespeare's play, and all the world around it. Not 'a rack', cloud or vapour will remain.

Everything is falling apart, coming to pieces, becoming 'indistinct', no longer 'visible'. It is happening as fast as thought ('even [just] with a thought'), as if thought itself were visible and visibly disappearing. Everything is evening. Antony is, 'even with a thought', '[e]ven such a body'. 'The rack dislimns': 'rack' here signifies the drifting clouds; 'dislimns' is apparently Shakespeare's invented negative for the verb 'to limn', meaning 'to paint'. 'Dislimns' would then have the sense of 'de-paints', 'paints out', 'effaces'. But it is difficult to read 'the rack dislimns' without construing in it the other sense of 'rack' (as torture 'rack') and a gruesome homophonic play on 'dislimns' as 'dislimbs'. Antony is evidently being torn to pieces. As he tells his 'knave' (boy or fellow) Eros, he 'cannot hold [the] visible shape' of Antony any longer. A cloud that is at one moment 'a horse' (the word 'like', we may notice, has by now completely evaporated) is already as 'indistinct / As water is in water'. In the final scene of *Antony and Cleopatra* this image of dissolving into water is to be hauntingly reiterated by Cleopatra's attendant, Charmian, as she witnesses her mistress dying: 'Dissolve, thick cloud, and rain, that I may say / The gods themselves do weep' (5.2.293–4).

Antony goes on, in Act 4 scene 14, to botch his own suicide, making an ignominious and agonizingly inefficient exit which nevertheless enables him to be at least briefly reconciled with his lover before death. Cleopatra is determined to die with him. In North's *Plutarch* we read of their Synapothanumenon ('signifying the order and agreement of those that will die together'), and of how thoroughly she has researched the least painful way of dying. Plutarch tells us that she has come to the conclusion that nothing works as well 'as the biting of an aspic, the which only causeth a heaviness of the head, without swounding or complaining, and bringeth a great desire also to sleep, with a little sweat in the face'. It is difficult not to imagine something like a ghostly nod inscribed in this image. In her act of dying Cleopatra seems to replay the scene of vanishing and dissolving evoked by Antony at the beginning of Act 4 scene 14, but in a fashion that leaves behind any of the negative connotations of being 'mock[ed] . . . with air'. She can no longer stay another moment. Just before the final nod, before her head drops and crown comes 'awry' (5.2.312), she voices a last, ecstatic affirmation of air itself, in other words of Antony:

> As sweet as balm, as soft as air, as gentle –
> O Antony! – Nay, I will take thee too.
> > [*She applies another asp*]
> What should I stay –   *Dies*
> > (5.2.305–7)

She does not finish her sentence. Charmian, questioningly, tries to: 'In this wild world?' (5.2.308). But it is with Cleopatra's aposiopesis, this joyous, nodding, erotic, mocking, unfinished affirmation that we might most aptly conclude this account of how to read Shakespeare: in mid-sentence, in mid-air.

NOTES

1 Thomas De Quincey, 'On the Knocking at the Gate in Macbeth' [1823], in *Romanticism: An Anthology*, 2nd ed., ed. Duncan Wu (Oxford: Blackwell, 1998), p. 640.

2 *Dr Johnson on Shakespeare*, ed. W. K. Wimsatt (Harmondsworth: Penguin, 1969), p. 68.

3 Samuel Beckett, *Murphy* (London: Picador: 1973), p. 41.

4 Friedrich Nietzsche, *Beyond Good and Evil: Prelude to a Philosophy of the Future*, trans. Walter Kaufmann (New York: Vintage, 1989), p. 93.

5 Lewis Carroll, *Alice's Adventures in Wonderland* and *Through the Looking-Glass* (New York: Signet, 1960), p. 63.

6 Elizabeth Bowen, 'Notes on Writing a Novel', in *Pictures and Conversations: Chapters of an Autobiography* (London: Allen Lane, 1975), p. 179.

7 Sigmund Freud, 'Some Character-Types Met with in Psychoanalytic Work', in *Pelican Freud Library*, vol. 14, trans. James Strachey, ed. Albert Dickson (Harmondsworth: Penguin, 1985), p. 308.

CHRONOLOGY

Note: Dates for the composition of Shakespeare's writings given here are those generally agreed among scholars, though they are also to varying degrees necessarily conjectural.

1564 26 April	baptized in Stratford-upon-Avon
1582 28 November	issue of marriage licence for William Shakespeare (aged 18) and Anne Hathaway (aged 26)
1583 26 May	Susanna, their daughter, baptized
1585 2 February	Judith and Hamnet, twin son and daughter, baptized
1590–91	*The Two Gentlemen of Verona, The Taming of the Shrew*
1591	*2 Henry VI, 3 Henry VI*
1592	Shakespeare referred to by Thomas Greene as an 'upstart crow' and 'the onely Shake-scene in a countrie'. *1 Henry VI, Titus Andronicus*
1592–3	*Richard III, Venus and Adonis*
1593–4	*The Rape of Lucrece*
1594	Shakespeare by this time a prominent member of the Lord Chamberlain's Men. *The Comedy of Errors*
1594–5	*Love's Labour's Lost*
1595	*Richard II, Romeo and Juliet, A Midsummer Night's Dream*
1596 11 August	burial of Hamnet Shakespeare (aged 11) in Stratford. *King John*
1596–7	*The Merchant of Venice, 1 Henry IV*
1597 4 May	Shakespeare buys New Place, Stratford

1597–8	*The Merry Wives of Windsor, 2 Henry IV*
1598	*Much Ado About Nothing*
1598–9	*Henry V*
1599	The Globe Theatre built. *Julius Caesar*
1599–1600	*As You Like It*
1600–1601	*Hamlet, Twelfth Night*
1601 8 September	burial of Shakespeare's father, John, in Stratford
1602 1 May	Shakespeare buys land in Old Stratford for £320. *Troilus and Cressida*
1593–1603	Composition of the Sonnets
1603 May	Shakespeare and other players become the King's Men. *Measure for Measure*
1603–4	*A Lover's Complaint, Sir Thomas More, Othello*
1604–5	*All's Well that Ends Well*
1605	*Timon of Athens*
1605–6	*King Lear*
1606	*Macbeth, Antony and Cleopatra*
1607 5 June	marriage of Susanna Shakespeare and John Hall. *Pericles*
1608 9 September	burial of Shakespeare's mother, Mary, in Stratford. *Coriolanus*
1609	*The Winter's Tale*, publication of *The Sonnets*
1610	*Cymbeline*
1611	*The Tempest*
1613 10 March	Shakespeare buys the Blackfriars Gatehouse, London.
29 June	Globe Theatre burns down. *Henry VIII*
1613–14	*The Two Noble Kinsmen* (with John Fletcher)
1616 10 February	marriage of Judith Shakespeare and Thomas Quiney
25 March	Shakespeare's will drawn up in Stratford
25 April	burial of Shakespeare in Stratford
1623 8 August	burial of Anne Shakespeare in Stratford. Publication of the First Folio

SUGGESTIONS FOR FURTHER READING

The most crucial thing is to have a good edition of the primary text. Versions of plays and poems published in the New Cambridge Shakespeare (under the current general editorship of Brian Gibbons), the Arden Shakespeare (3rd series, under the general editorship of Richard Proudfoot, Ann Thompson and David Scott Kastan) and the Oxford Shakespeare (Oxford World's Classics, under the general editorship of Stanley Wells) are consistently excellent. Every volume in these series is extremely helpful in providing a historical and critical context for the play or poetry in question, discussion of issues of staging and performance, and a carefully edited primary text, as well as clear and detailed notes and critical commentary, including information about differences between one early printed version and another. If you are looking for a single-volume collected works, the best option would be *The Norton Shakespeare*, edited by Stephen Greenblatt, Walter Cohen, Jean E. Howard and Katharine Eisaman Maus (1997), *The Riverside Shakespeare*, edited by G. Blakemore Evans (2nd edition, 1997), or *The RSC Shakespeare*, edited by Jonathan Bate and Eric Rasmussen (2007). All of these volumes provide a good deal of invaluable information and critical material, as well as extensive explanatory notes on the texts of the plays and poems themselves. Finally, for a particularly rich and probing edition of the

Sonnets, see *Shakespeare's Sonnets*, edited by Stephen Booth (Yale, 1977).

There are several very good series of critical work on Shakespeare. There is a Routledge series called Accents on Shakespeare, under the general editorship of Terence Hawkes: titles include *Philosophical Shakespeares*, edited by John J. Joughin, *Shakespeare Without Women* by Dympna Callaghan, *Shakespeare in Psychoanalysis* by Philip Armstrong, and *Post-Colonial Shakespeares*, edited by Ania Loomba and Martin Orkin. Oxford Shakespeare Topics is another adventurous and valuable series (general editors Peter Holland and Stanley Wells) with titles including *Shakespeare and the Bible* by Steven Marx, *Shakespeare and Eastern Europe* by Zdeněk Stříbrný, *Shakespeare's Reading* by Robert Miola, and *Shakespeare and Masculinity* by Bruce R. Smith. The Palgrave New Casebooks series includes numerous volumes on individual Shakespeare plays as well as, for example, *Shakespeare on Film*, edited by Robert Shaughnessy, *Shakespeare, Feminism and Gender*, edited by Kate Chedgzoy and *Shakespeare in Performance*, edited by Robert Shaughnessy. For an extensive anthology of some of the most influential recent critical work on Shakespeare, see *Shakespeare: An Anthology of Criticism and Theory 1945–2000*, edited by Russ McDonald (Blackwell, 2004).

For a fine single-volume collection of essays dealing with such topics as 'Shakespeare's life', 'What did Shakespeare read?', 'Playhouses, players, and playgoers in Shakespeare's time', 'Gender and sexuality in Shakespeare', 'Shakespeare and cinema', 'Shakespeare criticism' and 'Shakespeare reference books', see *The Cambridge Companion to Shakespeare*, edited by Margreta de Grazia and Stanley Wells (Cambridge University Press, 2001). For the meanings of specific words in Shakespeare, see C. T. Onions's invaluable glossary, published as *A Shakespeare Glossary* (revised edition by R. D. Eagleson, Oxford University Press, 1986). The *OED* (*Oxford English Dictionary*) (2nd edition, 1989; also available online on subscription at *www.oed.com*) gives especially close attention to words that appear in Shakespeare. For a single-volume English dictionary, *Chambers Dictionary* (9th edition, 2003) is admirably Shakespeare-oriented: many words are separately defined specifically in terms of their meanings in Shakespeare. For a Shakespeare concordance, the standard hard copy text is Marvin Spevack, *A Complete and Systematic Concordance to the Works of Shakespeare*, 8 vols. (Hildesheim, Georg Olms, 1968–75); alternatively, online, consult *www.languid.org/cgi-bin/shakespeare* or *www.it.usyd.edu.au/~matty/Shakespeare/*. On questions of metre and prosody, I would particularly recommend George T. Wright's *Shakespeare's Metrical Art* (University of California Press, 1989). It may sound dry as dust, but E. A. Abbott's *A Shakespearean Grammar: An Attempt to Illustrate Some of the Differences Between Elizabethan and Modern English* (3rd edition, 1870; reprinted Dover Publications, 2003), originally written for Victorian public schoolboys, remains a rich and deeply informative study. On sexual wordplay in Shakespeare, see Eric Partridge, *Shakespeare's Bawdy* (1947; reprinted Routledge Classics, 2001) or, for a more recent account, Gordon Williams, *A Glossary of Shakespeare's Sexual Language* (Athlone Press, 1997).

For a couple of recent wide-ranging critical studies that are especially thought provoking, as well as good on the poetic dimensions of Shakespeare's writing, see Harold Bloom's *Shakespeare: The Invention of the Human* (Fourth Estate, 1999) and Frank Kermode's *Shakespeare's Language* (Penguin, 2000). Of related interest, particularly regarding the importance of the literary or writerly character of Shakespeare's work, see

Lukas Erne, *Shakespeare as Literary Dramatist* (Cambridge University Press, 2003).

For two excellent biographical accounts of Shakespeare, see Samuel Schoenbaum, *William Shakespeare: A Documentary Life* (Clarendon Press, 1975), and Park Honan, *Shakespeare: A Life* (Oxford University Press, 1998). More recently, James Shapiro's *1599: A Year in the Life of Shakespeare* (Faber, 2005) offers a remarkable evocation of Shakespeare's writing and other activities in London that year, while Charles Nicholl's *The Lodger: Shakespeare on Silver Street* (Allen Lane, 2007) illuminates in new ways the period in and around 1604, when Shakespeare was renting a room in Cripplegate. In *Shakespeare in Company* (Oxford University Press, 2013), Bart van Es provides an original and compelling account of Shakespeare as a theatrical collaborator, working with and alongside actors, playwrights and others.

Finally, for some useful websites, see:

www.shakespeare.palomar.edu
www.folger.edu
www.shakespeare.org.uk
www.bl.uk/treasures/shakespeare/homepage.html
www.absoluteshakespeare.com

INDEX